JOSEPH RUHOMON'S
INDIA

INDIA;

The Progress of Her People at Home and Abroad,

And How Those in British Guiana May Improve Themselves;

BEING

A LECTURE

DELIVERED

IN ST. LEONARD'S SCHOOL ROOM, GEORGETOWN, DEMERARA,

On the Evening of the Fourth October, 1894,

AND NOW IN A PAMPHLET FORM, WITH SLIGHT IMPROVEMENTS;

PRESENTED TO THE PUBLIC BY

JOSEPH RUHOMON.

GEORGETOWN, DEMERARA:
C. K. JARDINE, PRINTER TO THE GOVERNMENT OF BRITISH GUIANA

Joseph Ruhomon's
India
The Progress of Her People at Home and Abroad, and How Those in British Guiana May Improve Themselves

Introduced with Notes and Appendices
by
Clem Seecharan

University of the West Indies Press
Barbados • Jamaica • Trinidad and Tobago

University of the West Indies Press
1A Aqueduct Flats   Mona
Kingston 7   Jamaica

© 2001 by Clem Seecharan
All rights reserved. Published 2001

05 04 03 02 01   5 4 3 2 1

CATALOGUING IN PUBLICATION DATA

Seecharan, Clem
   Joseph Ruhomon's India; the progress of her people at home and
   abroad, and how those in British Guiana may improve themselves /
   Clem Seecharan.
   p. cm.

   Partial contents: India; the progress of her people at home and abroad,
   and how those in British Guiana may improve themselves, being a
   lecture . . . / delivered by Joseph Ruhomon / previously published
   Georgetown, British Guiana: C. K. Jardine, 1894.

   Includes bibliographical references and index.
   ISBN: 976-640-095-4
   1. Ruhomon, Joseph, 1873–1942. 2. East Indians – Guyana.
   3. Guyana – History. 4. India – History. I. Ruhomon, Joseph,
   1873–1942. II. Title. III. Title: India; the progress of her people at
   home and abroad.

   F2391.E2 S46 2001   988.1'004914

   Cover and book design by Alan Ross

To Rajkishore Mangal,

my great teacher

CONTENTS

Acknowledgements viii
Foreword ix

PART 1
CHAPTER ONE
Joseph Ruhomon and the Making of *India* . . .
1

CHAPTER TWO
H.V.P. Bronkhurst and Joseph Ruhomon:
The Shaping of an Intellect
11

CHAPTER THREE
On Reading *India; The Progress of Her People
at Home and Abroad*: Some Contextual Thoughts
19

Notes to Part 1
34

PART 2
The Lecture
45

Notes to Part 2
71

Appendices I–VI 79
Bibliography 94
Index 97

ACKNOWLEDGEMENTS

I am grateful to Frank Birbalsingh, Bridget Brereton, Rita Christian, Peter Fraser, Kusha Haraksingh, Denis Judd, Brij Lal, Brinsley Samaroo, Mary Turner and Donald Wood for their friendship and scholarly example; Jack Balder, Andrew Bishop, Sarran Jagmohan, Ian McDonald and Roopram Ramharack for taking an interest in my work and for telling me that it is important; Mazrul Bacchus and Roy Sawh for unfailing comradeship; Helen Nelson for the typing; and Chris for believing in me.

FOREWORD

In political terms, with two major exceptions, the 1890s were everywhere particularly bleak for people who were not of European descent. In the United States of America, the end of Reconstruction allowed white supremacist governments to disenfranchise African Americans; the partition of Africa and the extension of imperial control globally, made the imperial powers appear unusually secure and invulnerable. Even the two exceptions seemed to confirm this superiority: the Ethiopian defeat of the Italian invasion had been the last triumph of traditional Africa; the Japanese success against China (and soon against Russia) depended on imitating Europe. Yet Joseph Ruhomon, whose 1894 pamphlet is here reissued in an excellent new edition by Dr Clem Seecharan, proved to be part of a larger movement of ideas ultimately subversive of that triumphant colonialism.

Of immediate importance to the topic of Ruhomon's pamphlet, had been the founding of the Indian National Congress in 1885. The influence that this organization would have, throughout the British Empire, must not be underestimated. The Indian subcontinent had replaced the Caribbean as the central possession of the British Empire at the beginning of the nineteenth century: the movement towards independence would have a greater effect in dissolving the British Empire than had the independence of the thirteen British North American colonies in the late eighteenth century. The example of the Indian struggle for independence, and the effect of its achievement in 1947, would unravel the Empire on which the sun never set, in a remarkably short time. The pride in his heritage that Ruhomon displays was one shared by many equally young people in India, and would play a crucial role in those struggles.

Outside India, similar movements of intellectual resistance to the racist pretensions of Europe were stirring. The creoles of Sierra Leone had already begun to produce writers like James Africanus Horton who, as early as 1868, had sought to vindicate the African race. People of African descent from the Americas, like Alexander Crummell of the United States and Edward Blyden of the Danish Virgin Islands, asserted the potential of Africans based on their experience of living in Africa, and wrote of their past achievements. Within the Caribbean itself, such voices also existed. The Haitian élite had fought a long intellectual war after independence, one in which their admiration for French civilization did not prevent their claiming racial equality. In the second Cuban war for independence (1895–1898), a Cuban of African descent, Antonio Maceo, was one of the leading generals. The British Caribbean did not lag far behind.

In the British Caribbean, the weight of British colonialism had become heavier after the Morant Bay Rebellion of 1865. Jamaica had lost its system of representative government, and throughout the Eastern Caribbean, too, the Crown Colony system that postponed indefinitely the prospect of wider political participation, spread. By the end of the century, black Jamaicans, most notably Robert Love and T.E.S. Scholes, had begun to denounce British colonialism. Trinidad had been the pioneer of Crown Colony government; Trinidad also possessed a group of educated and articulate opponents of the system: J.J. Thomas would prove to be the most profoundly radical of all. In 1869, he published his book on Trinidad creole, the earliest recognition in the British Caribbean that the culture of the masses had intrinsic value. By the late 1880s, Thomas was the best known of those repudiating the arguments of J.A. Froude on the inferiority of Caribbean people. By the early 1890s, a younger contemporary, F.A. Durham, was advocating fleeing British colonialism and building up Liberia and by the late 1890s, Durham's brothers, with another Trinidadian, Henry Sylvester Williams, had founded in London the African Association, which would lead to the Pan-African Conference of 1900.

In Guyana, at that time, the dominance of the sugar interests and the difficulty that the majority of the people faced in making a living concentrated minds on questions of political economy, whether the wider social ones or the narrower ones of individual advancement. Joseph Ruhomon's criticisms need to be read in that light, recalling those of J.R. Moore written twenty years before. Moore was concerned about the failure of Afro-Guyanese to emulate their ancestors who had displayed all the Victorian virtues in their response to emancipation. Like Ruhomon, Moore saw these faults as individual, not innate. Both Moore and Ruhomon understood what the Japanese had learnt: one either imitated or one became subordinated. But Ruhomon also looked forward.

The Japanese had been determined to imitate Europe without becoming imitation Europeans. The twentieth century would see the development, in both the African and Indian diasporas, of similar beliefs. In the seven years from 1929 to 1935, three Guyanese would publish works that would attempt to entrench these beliefs. Norman Cameron published his *Evolution of the Negro*, dealing with the history of Africa and Afro-Guyanese; the Tobagonian immigrant, A.R.F. Webber, his *Centenary History*, a history consciously not from the planters' perspective; and Ayube Edun his *London's Heart-Probe*, both a proposal for the reconstruction of the British Empire and the statement of his political philosophy, which would guide the Man Power Citizens' Association, the first sugar workers' union in British Guiana. A dozen years later, Joseph Ruhomon's brother, Peter, would publish his history of the Indo-Guyanese, in Guyana. All these later works would attempt to celebrate modernity and cultural distinctiveness. In 1894 Joseph Ruhomon did both with a generosity of spirit that should shame any Guyanese reflecting on the last four decades of our history. In that respect, a return to Victorian values reinterpreted by that late nineteenth-century generation who rejected the "scientific racism" of Europe might help Guyana of the twenty-first century. Joseph Ruhomon would have hoped so.

Peter Fraser
Goldsmith's College
University of London

PART 1
CHAPTER ONE

Joseph Ruhomon and the Making of *India*

INTRODUCTION

... "coolies" we called them, whether they were labourers or eventually became doctors or barristers or Civil Servants.

– Edgar Mittelholzer, *A Swarthy Boy*

In general, the Indian tradition renders a favourable opinion of the intellectual. The Indian intellectual is the heir of the Brahmins, he is the successor of the pundits.

– Edward Shils, *The Intellectual between Tradition and Modernity: The Indian Situation*

We have to thank Mr Joseph Ruhomon for a report of the lecture which he recently delivered in St Leonard's School-room, entitled:- "India: The Progress of her People at Home and Abroad; and how those in British Guiana may improve Themselves", which has been printed in pamphlet form.

Daily Chronicle, 28 December 1894

Joseph Ruhomon (1873–1942) was the first Indian intellectual in British Guiana (Guyana). He was a man with a passion for the pursuit of reason.[1] It is true that as he grew older his Christianity was paraded more frequently, often getting in the way of his logic; but it was a non-proselytizing Christianity, aimed at the lessening of moral and material poverty, and never supercilious or denigrating to "non-believers".

Indian indentureship in the Caribbean – the badge of inferiority and shame of self – had begun, in 1838, in British Guiana. Fifty years after and beyond, Indians in the colony were still seen as "coolies",[2] a pejorative term which encapsulated notions of servitude, ignorance, heathenism and barbarism – the new slave in late nineteenth century British Guiana. Most indentured labourers, as well as "free coolies" and their children, were illiterate. For the small minority who thought they had eluded the consuming "coolie" persona, this unflattering image lingered, a stain on real progress and visions of expanding possibilities. There were still, in the 1890s, very few Indian professionals: school teachers, civil servants, clerical people on sugar estates.[3] There were no Indo-Guyanese legislators, doctors or lawyers; no university-educated people. In short, there was an absence of an intellectual tradition, no star by which to steer.

This pamphlet, *India; The Progress of Her People at Home and Abroad*, published in December 1894, is the first extended piece published by an Indo-Guyanese; it is, indeed, the first by an Indian in the Caribbean. Over one hundred years ago, Joseph Ruhomon, aged only twenty-one, undertook an intellectual scrutiny of the Indian condition in British Guiana. Nothing like this had ever been done by an Indian in the region. And, in an age when the "coolie" shadow quickly clouded vision and self-deprecation was an instinct, the construction of this essay was an admirable accomplishment.[4] It belongs to the Caribbean intellectual tradition, an achievement of all the people.

Ruhomon's timely, rehabilitative intent, the pursuit of intimations of ancestral greatness, his sensitivity to the cultural diversity of the Colony, his magnanimity of spirit, and his reprimand of his Indo-Guyanese compatriots for not cultivating the intellect, reflect a bewildering precocity worthy of a mature scholar-statesman. Although the tenor of his reprimand is often severe, it betrays youthful impetuosity, an impatience which could not comprehend the context of Indian struggles in plantation society, nor accommodate the small, often imperceptible, efforts of a new community as they meandered to incremental material betterment and a reshaped identity.

But Ruhomon's treatise is not mired in despair or sterile spite. Impelled by an amazing grasp of Indian history, and by contemporary changes in the "motherland", India, he believed that the status of Indians in British Guiana could be transformed in the same way that India was being metamorphosed through its contact with Britain – a process he also identified and commended among Africans at home and in the diaspora.

Who was this prodigy, Joseph Ruhomon? What were the forces which shaped his intellect? How was *India; The Progress of Her People at Home and Abroad* shaped by the local and wider environments?

Biographical Note: A Study in Integrity

Joseph Ruhomon belonged to one of the most distinguished families in British Guiana but came from a branch of it which has not been adequately recognized.[5] He was born on 2 August 1873 at Plantation Albion, on the Corentyne Coast, in the county of Berbice. His father, John Ruhomon (Ruhoman), had been taken to British Guiana as an indentured labourer in 1859, aged eleven. He was accompanied by his brothers, Pahalad, aged thirteen, and Lokhooa (Moses Luckhoo), aged seven. Nothing is known of their parents in India: the boys were picked up in Lucknow, United Provinces, and enticed to go as "bound coolies" to Demerara [British Guiana]. They were probably promised the world.

Pahalad remained a Hindu all his life (he died in November 1921);[6] but Ruhoman and Lokhooa converted to Christianity, early, and were named John Ruhoman and Moses Luckhoo, respectively. The fact that these boys, apparently, had lost all contact with their parents or any other members of their extended family, paradoxically, became an advantage in British Guiana. They could dream big and follow uncharted paths, fed by their young, volatile imaginations; untrammelled by the protective, but inhibiting, certainties of the Indian family. Because Ruhoman and Lokhooa came under missionary influence early, they appreciated the power of western education while still young; they embraced it without equivocation or self-doubt. Moreover, their adaptation to the colony was more rapid because they probably experienced no lingering prevarication fed by the longing to return to the "motherland", nor illusory thoughts prompted by the call of a lost paradise. British Guiana was home; the effort could be concentrated and single-minded.

John Ruhoman, Joseph's father, mastered English and was equally competent in Hindi, while acquiring some facility in Tamil and Urdu. So although he became a Christian, his linguistic proficiency still kept some of his roots in his ancestral tradition. This gave him the self-confidence to achieve in creole society, to transcend the limitations bred by perceptions of the "coolie". He qualified, locally, as a sick-nurse and dispenser, chemist and druggist,[7] and a dentist. He also developed leadership skills: for several years he held senior administrative positions at various plantation hospitals, Albion, Port Mourant, Smithfield, before he opened a drug-store in New Amsterdam, the main town in Berbice.

Moses Luckhoo, also, was educated in English, and was taught Hindi by John Ruhomon. He qualified as an interpreter and worked for many years in that capacity, at the magistrate's court in New Amsterdam, a contact with the law which profoundly influenced the professional direction of his own nuclear family. Luckhoo married well: his wife, Elizabeth Saywack, was the daughter of a very successful Indo-Guyanese businessman in New Amsterdam. He worked for a while in his father-in-law's business before opening his own provision store. Later, he started a dry goods store in the same town. His progress was inexorable.

Dwarka Nath suggests that Pahalad, the eldest brother, was the bedrock on which the success of the extended family was built. A resourceful man who retained his Hindu faith, he provided the psychological and initial financial mooring for his younger brothers, John and Moses, to embark on their early careers with some security and self-confidence. The old responsibility within the Indian joint family had survived the crossing.

Moses Luckhoo and his wife, Elizabeth, fortified by commercial success, were among the first Indians in British Guiana able to send at least some of their sons to Queen's College, the élite secondary school in Georgetown. Three of their five sons attended Queen's. One of them, E.A. Luckhoo, became the first Indo-Guyanese solicitor, in 1899;[8] another, J.A. Luckhoo, became the first Indo-Guyanese to qualify as a lawyer, in England in 1912;[9] while David Lawrence Luckhoo, who had worked as a dispenser with his uncle, John Ruhomon, became a medical doctor, having studied at the Universities of Toronto, Edinburgh and Glasgow.[10] Their son Henry Adolphus, having started out as a salesman in the family business, later became a clerk in J.A. Luckhoo's legal chambers; while the fifth son, Samuel Thomas, managed the business after his father's death. Moses and Elizabeth's daughter, Amy Eliza, who also worked in the business, was married to Edgar Adams, the first Indo-Guyanese public auditor. Many of their grandchildren and great-grandchildren have also achieved legal eminence.

Joseph Ruhomon and the Making of *India*

John Ruhomon does not seem to have achieved the same measure of commercial success; and his sons, Joseph Ruhomon (born 1873) and Peter Ruhomon (born 1880), did not have the opportunity to be professionally trained overseas. Joseph became a journalist, while Peter worked the laborious, measured way up, in the colonial civil service. In the context of their own voraciously upwardly mobile extended family, and an Indian community immersed in the daily grind for a degree of financial security, with its narrow, materialistic ethos, these were minor achievements. Law and medicine were the élite professions bearing magical associations even among illiterate Indians: they brought instant financial rewards; they facilitated considerable independence of the plantocracy and the colonial state, still prejudiced by obstinate, racial perceptions of colonial peoples and their supposed innate incapacity for leadership and responsibility.[11] These professions were seen as big jobs, white people's work, yielding tangible, powerful results.

It is arguable that the clearly less enthusiastic perception among the Indo-Guyanese concerning professions such as teaching, journalism and the civil service hurt Joseph and Peter Ruhomon. It tended to diminish their seminal achievements. This lack of affirmation from their community probably fed an undercurrent of envy towards the Luckhoos and other successful Indians who, especially after World War I, rose impressively in the acclaimed professions and business.

It is noteworthy that many African and coloured (mixed race) people in British Guiana, with no roots in agriculture or commerce, identified the so-called ordinary professions as important instruments of mobility. Indeed, their dominance in teaching and the lower echelons of the civil service, by the 1880s–90s, had erased much of the stigma of slavery and enhanced their stature in creole society.[12] Joseph Ruhomon, therefore, became even more committed to the pursuit of the intellect, to the use of knowledge and reason, to challenge colonial assumptions. *India; The Progress of Her People at Home and Abroad* may be seen as the watershed in the transformation of the Indo-Guyanese psyche. The Indo-Guyanese, for the first time, mounts an intellectual challenge of creole society's calumniation of him; uses the language and the scholarly instruments of the colonizer (as his compatriots in India were already doing) to begin to gnaw away at the deep-rooted construct, "the coolie" – that embodiment which spoke of menial jobbing and a multitude of associations of coarseness, reserved for all Indians whatever their situation.

In fact, Joseph Ruhomon, for nearly fifty years until his death in 1942, argued unceasingly that Indians in British Guiana could not really be deemed to have progressed until they had cultivated the intellect, and gained a moral and spiritual excellence – a generosity of spirit fed by reason and control of the emotions. He deprecated what he saw as unbridled selfishness, absence of responsibility beyond family and a general unresponsiveness to broader societal goals; an obsession with material success in a social void.[13]

In March 1924, nearly thirty years after *India; The Progress of Her People at Home and Abroad*, Joseph Ruhomon, addressing the Christian Indian Society of New Amsterdam, commended the example of a respected, late Indo-Guyanese businessman, J.W. Permaul of Rose Hall, Corentyne. He reportedly exhorted his compatriots thus:

They should not imagine that they were in the world to serve their own petty interest or the interest of their narrow family circle. Mr. Permaul was a public-spirited man and manifested a keen interest in the progress and welfare of the masses . . . He could intelligently and sympathetically enter into the discussion of any aspect of colonial affairs . . .[14]

Earlier, in 1921, the year after all Indian indentures were cancelled in the colony, Joseph Ruhomon had made a plea for moral consciousness beyond self and family. While acknowledging the achievements of Indo-Guyanese as rice farmers, cattle-rearers and shopkeepers, as well as their admirable progress in many technical jobs on the sugar plantations, he bemoaned what he considered their imperviousness to communal responsibility. He wrote with evident passion:

It is the duty of the strong to help the weak, as much as it is the rightful moral demand of the weak to have the assistance of the strong. Those [Indians], however, who have got to the top of the ladder either through their own efforts or with the adventitious aid of good fortune, have always been loathe to recognise their obligations in this respect . . . Many . . . armed with all the power for good represented by a superabundance of cash, have often been appealed to by well-meaning reformers for the wherewithal to organise and operate for the general welfare, but to no avail. Appeals of this kind at once bring the idolised self looming so largely before them that everything else on the horizon of a wider and nobler life is completely shut out from view . . . "What am I to get for it?" is the question immediately asked by the party appealed to.[15]

Joseph Ruhomon's broader sympathies, probably, were shaped by his boyhood on the two Corentyne plantations, where his father was a chemist and druggist. At one of these estates, Albion, owned by the Campbell family since the days of slavery, Jock Campbell recalls, following his first visit there in 1934, that mules were kept better than coolies, because, he was told, mules cost more to replace than coolies.[16] Conditions at Port Mourant, the other estate where Ruhomon's father worked, were infinitely better: it was an organized place, where Indians were allocated well-watered plots to grow rice and communal areas to rear cattle. Indians at Port Mourant acquired a greater sense of belonging and pride of place. This bred an independence of spirit, even a perceptibly rebellious temper.[17] But generally the Corentyne estates, with a drier, more salubrious climate on this sprawling, wind-swept coast, were healthier and less malarial than the riverine estates and those on the wetter Demerara and Essequibo Coasts.[18]

Slightly better economic conditions on the Corentyne Coast, coupled with better health, shaped a more assertive, self-confident Indian. Joseph Ruhomon was a product of this environment; he was the highest manifestation of this new spirit, already discernible in the early 1890s. In his case, this focus acquired sharper definition by the fact that his father, John Ruhomon, represented the first sprinkling of Indians who were located in the middle strata of the estate hierarchical order. He did not do menial, "coolie" work; and he could hold his own with any man, of any race.[19]

This rebellious streak would have been quickened and sustained by the persistence of the "bound coolie" image throughout indentureship and beyond.[20] But Joseph Ruhomon was the first Indo-Guyanese, until he was joined by Bechu in the late 1890s, with the intellectual gifts and courage to articulate the Indian condition. As an observer remarked, "The superstructure of his education was extensive reading based on the solidity of a sound secondary education."[21] He could have added that this education was rooted in deep Christian principles, an uncompromising pursuit of the truth, fearlessness in challenging the goliaths of privilege and colonial complacency. This was what fed his frequently provocative correspondence in the press and his radical journalism in the first decade of this century when, as editor of the weekly, the *People*, in New Amsterdam, he was a resolute champion of both Indo- and Afro-Guyanese workers, an implacable foe of the plantocracy and its many allies in colonial Guyana.[22]

Joseph Ruhomon also believed in what, in his 1894 lecture, the precursor to *India; The Progress of Her People at Home and Abroad*, he called "the potency and influence of the platform".[23] This established a pattern in his intellectual work. He would usually deliver a series of lectures to the public in his home town, New Amsterdam, or to an Indian organization in Georgetown. Invariably, these would be serialized or covered copiously in the local press. Shortly afterwards, he would revise the lectures and publish them as pamphlets. This is the pattern discernible in the many pamphlets that appeared: *India; The Progress of Her People at Home and Abroad; Records of the Past; Good and Evil; Signs and Portents; The Transitory and the Permanent; The Higher Evolution; Reminiscences of Old Berbice;* and *The Marvel of the Ages*. A man of the world of books, he invited all, men and women, to share the pleasures of his world. As he remarked in 1894: "Books are one of the greatest blessings in life, and the educated mind which dives into literature, enjoys a pleasure of which the rude uncultured mind knows nothing" (p. 69).

It is noteworthy that, by the 1890s, the Berbice Library in New Amsterdam provided readers with an impressive range of good books; it also had an ongoing lecture series, feeding the curiosity of its young members. Joseph Ruhomon was a principal beneficiary of this opportunity.[24] Walter Rodney believes that at the turn of the twentieth century New Amsterdam had become "the virtual political capital of the country". He attributes this primarily to the work of a radical Congregational minister in the town, Revd H.J. Shirley, an Englishman who, between 1900 and 1903, was an articulate, fearless champion of the working people, whatever their race. An unconquerable foe of colonial bigotry and the narrowness of privilege, he founded a radical weekly, the *People*, in September 1901. Ruhomon's way of seeing was congruent with Shirley's uncompromising partiality for the underdog.[25]

A few months after Shirley arrived in New Amsterdam in July 1900, he wrote to the *Birmingham Post* on the injustices meted out to Indian workers on the estates. He observed:

If an overseer kicks a coolie into a trench . . . the coolie has no remedy but what he takes in his own hands. Let him, however, strike an overseer and a batch of policemen are sent off to arrest him, and he is severely sentenced to prison . . . There is an immigration agency which costs the country some thousands a year, and is supposed to secure them justice, but supposition is not always paralleled with fact.[26]

Ruhomon absorbed this passion for justice, a foundation of his Christian principles. In December 1901, reflecting on Christ's mission, he argued: "[T]he great Galilean's work was not merely to establish a Church, but to make mankind happier and better . . . The principles of love, justice, liberty, retribution, and the general conduct of life which He laid down are truths as fixed and as stable as the eternal hills . . ."[27]

It was this tradition of fairness and fearlessness which Ruhomon took to his several journalistic engagements. (Some time after the authorities forced Shirley to leave British Guiana, in 1903, Ruhomon became editor of the *People*.) In 1908 he was appointed a sub-editor of the *Daily Argosy*; later he was a feature writer of the *Daily Chronicle* and its Berbice representative; then the founder of the short-lived *Indian Opinion* in 1917; and a co-editor of a small paper, the *Demerara Standard*. Towards the end of his life, his integrity as a writer had earned him many honorifics: "The Doyen of Local Journalists"; "The Dean of Local Authors".[28] When he died on 16 September 1942, aged sixty-nine, the *Daily Chronicle* noted that only a few hours before he had completed another pamphlet, "Facts and Factors in World Drama or the Passing of the Old Order". The proceeds from its sale would go to the Red Cross Fund. The paper added: "A man who possessed a wealth of knowledge, Mr. Ruhomon was . . . one of the country's most modest and unassuming characters."[29]

As he grew older, Joseph Ruhomon's Christian principles tended to obtrude; but there was always evidence in his thoughts of omnivorous reading as well as compassion and tolerance pitted against crass materialism, obscurantism, national chauvinism, and racial arrogance fed by the superiority of so-called civilized peoples. After the savagery of "civilized" man in the Boer War and in World War I, he inveighed against narrow conceptions of progress rooted in spiralling materialism and greed.[30] Modesty, moral responsibility and "ethical goodness" were at the core of Ruhomon's vision of the civilized life. As he argued in his lecture, "The Transitory and the Permanent", to the Wesleyan East Indian Young Men's Society in Georgetown in 1922: "The decay and destruction of all past civilizations was due not to the dwindling of knowledge, but to the corruption of morals." Ruhomon extended this to explain what he saw as the contemporary "curse of Europe":

The spirit involved a hatred of other nationalities and a desire to grow great, powerful, wealthy and dominant at their expense. It was an absorbing, consuming, insatiable passion guided by no moral laws and restrained by no moral restrictions. At its root was racial pride and an overweening conceit, a consciousness of superiority over other races and therefore an utter contempt of them and of their rights.[31]

Who was this Indo-Guyanese prodigy, Joseph Ruhomon? The *Daily Chronicle*, in their obituary published on 23 September 1942, was most discerning:

The achievements of a man's life are . . . reckoned by the public in terms of offices held, books written, honours won; but a man's friends, such as the many Joseph Ruhomon had, made a more intimate reckoning. In his company one felt that life was a glorious adventure, full of possibilities.

CHAPTER TWO

H.V.P. Bronkhurst and Joseph Ruhomon: The Shaping of an Intellect

Two Sundays ago I went on a sugar estate . . . to preach and there I was mortified to see four Coolie converts, members of our Church, in whom I had great confidence, taking part in a heathenish festival and having on their foreheads the emblem of heathenism. When spoken to, they felt ashamed, and did not, however, think there was any harm done inasmuch [as] some other Christians . . . in other places, did the same . . . On another estate I was told by a few if I could find nothing to do, come and speak to them about this rubbish religion called Christianity. They could all, at once, become Christians if I could speak to the Governor and obtain for them first class situations, lands, and houses. I was on three occasions asked how much the Government paid me for making Christians . . . of the Coolies.

– Revd H.V.P. Bronkhurst to the General Secretaries, Wesleyan Mission House, London, 30 November 1877

Probably the most profound intellectual influence on Joseph Ruhomon, in the late 1880s and early 1890s, was Revd H.V.P. Bronkhurst (1826–1895), Wesleyan missionary to the Indians in British Guiana from 1860 to 1895. Ruhomon had worked briefly as an "issuer" at the public hospital and the alms house in Georgetown, in the early 1890s. When Bronkhurst died in Georgetown on 17 July 1895,[32] Joseph Ruhomon acknowledged his debt to him, "as one who on several occasions had been privileged to sit by his side and to listen to his words of wisdom . . . words that have always inspired and nerved my heart". He added that he and many of his Indo-Guyanese compatriots had been "influenced for good", and held "respectable positions" in the colony, because of the work and "sterling character" of this "great lover of his countrymen and their off-spring",[33] Henry Valentine Peter Bronkhurst. Who was this man? How did he influence Joseph Ruhomon?

Bronkhurst was born on 21 March 1826 in Tanjore District (Madras), in South India.[34] He was a Eurasian: Dutch on his father's side, Tamil on his mother's. In spite of his Christian upbringing, he was exposed to various strands in the complex religious tradition of India and was, by the age of fourteen, already proficient in several Indian languages. Bronkhurst was especially fascinated by that celebrated, ancient book of the Aryans, the *Rig-Veda*. By the time he left India in 1842, for a brief stay in Australia, he could empathize with many facets of the rich ancient Indian heritage being unearthed by Western scholars since the late eighteenth century, as well as with the intellectual awakening best exemplified by the great Bengali reformer, Ram Mohan Roy (1770–1833).

Bronkhurst's Christian faith, meanwhile, was deepened by a three-year sojourn in the Holy Land – an experience which, for the rest of his life, provided a fount of anecdotal gems that enriched his sermons and lectures. When he died, it was noted that "[h]e was a keen observer of men and customs, with an eye for everything that could prove in the least interesting, and was always ready to give others the benefit of his extensive knowledge and learning in an unassuming and unostentatious way".[35] It was a learning rooted in the diversity of peoples and the peculiarities of places.

From Palestine, Bronkhurst had gone to England where for some years he taught Syriac, Sanskrit and Hebrew. So he combined his magnificent proficiency in Eastern languages with daunting erudition in secular and ecclesiastical subjects: history, etymology and theology. He was, by the 1850s, already an intellectual by temperament. The 1850s, with its Victorian imperialistic certainties and robust, evangelical Christianity, quickened the missionary instincts in Bronkhurst. In late December 1860 he arrived in British Guiana to succeed the late Revd J.E.S. Williams who, since 1852, had been the first Wesleyan Methodist missionary to the Indians.

Bronkhurst's background fitted him eminently for this task but after six years he had converted only sixteen Indians. As late as the early 1880s this dedicated proselytizer's message was still falling on stony ground: the harvest of "coolie" converts was still paltry. The despair showed; the resilience, the implacability of Hindus and Muslims (the latter even more so), in the face of an avalanche of Christian missionaries, received copious attention in Bronkhurst's voluminous writings in the 1870s and 1880s.[36] He observed:

[T]heir religion exercises a prodigious influence over the people ... Blind adherence is paid to this cursed system. The Coolies deem it as perilous to forsake their religion as for a locomotive to quit the line. Whatever may be thought by others of the absurdity of the thing, they nevertheless sincerely believe in the divinity of a dumb idol. The evidence of their senses goes for nothing in the face of time-honoured and hoary tradition.[37]

Later, reflecting on the massive literary heritage of the Hindus, Bronkhurst was even more uncharitable in the opprobrium he vented, dismissing it thus:

[T]he standard writings of the Hindus are so filled with exaggerated, impossible, improbable, monstrous, and unreliable romances and fictions, written by (unprincipled and) cunning or designing men, with a view to raise themselves in importance at the expense of truth and justice, by depreciating those inimical to them, that not much reliance can be placed on what these writings contain or say ... One cannot read the ancient Hindu books without profound pity that the human mind should become so deceitful as to invent, or so degraded as to accept, such monstrous falsehoods and absurdities. The chronology, geography, ethnology, and theology of India are a farrago of deception and superstition.[38]

As late as 1931, over seventy years after Bronkhurst began his missionary labours among the Indians of British Guiana, only 11,195 in a population of 130,540, were reported to be Christians[39] – many, possibly, nominally so. It was common to submit to conversion in an effort to procure a teaching job in the denominational schools. Only 741 Indians were returned as Methodists in 1931.[40] One can comprehend the roots of Bronkhurst's despair.

However, it would be wrong to assess Bronkhurst's work in British Guiana by the paucity of his converts, or the seemingly bigoted, vitriolic tenor of his response to the intransigence of the "heathens". Indeed, there are two discernible strands in his understanding of the Indian legacy. The more enlightened one contributed, in British Guiana, to an appreciation of another dimension of India's heritage – the ancient, Aryan and Hindu, secular achievements of compelling artistic opulence and excellence, the gifts of a civilized people in the very remote past. This would have triggered a resurgent pride in Ruhomon's Indianness, an antithesis to the universe of the despised "coolie".[41]

The other strand was rooted in the arrogant, intolerant, obsessively evangelical soil of Victorian Christianity with its assumption of a divine mission to rescue "natives" from barbarism and heathenism. From this position, therefore, no one but the satanic could embrace Hinduism, as Bronkhurst argued in the late 1880s:

No man's life can be right whose faith is wrong. A man's life can only be right when his faith is right. It is quite evident that Hinduism – the religion professed by a larger majority of our East Indian Immigrants – is not true, and cannot be true, and therefore their *life* cannot be right. It is a religion which cannot be improved. It is corrupt to the very core. Its essential principles are founded in error.[42]

This gracelessness seems even more offensive coming from an Anglo-Indian. But it is comprehensible when one recognizes that deep-seated ethnic and cultural insecurities were what defined the Anglo-Indian in the Indian environment. Never accepted fully by Europeans in India, deemed an outcaste by caste-obsessed Indians, this gnawing inbetweenity which spoke of placelessness, bred a passion to appropriate the idioms, to parade the acquired traits, of their putative European protectors. It was crucial to their survival, material and psychological, to earn some recognition from the ruling race: the tendency to ape British manners and beliefs, however ineptly, answered the need, the necessity, to distance themselves from their Indian roots. It also bred a tendency to deprecate the latter in a somewhat exaggeratedly affected way. It was as if the barbarism of the Indian horde would promptly claw back intimations of civility, of superiority, cultivated on the long, slippery road to a kind of Britishness.[43]

It was this narrow, intolerant strand in Bronkhurst's thoughts which led him, time and again, to deprecate coolie behaviour. Unwittingly, he stimulated a response from one or two Indian correspondents, as early as 1882, thus initiating a tradition of critical letter-writing to the press, in defence of Indian interests. On 22 March 1882, in the first instalment of his unsigned article, "The Character and Manner of Living of the Coolies in the Colony", he had argued that he found some coolies to be "cunning . . . some of them are very vicious . . . while in others, we find falsehood, duplicity, apathy, selfishness, avarice, sensuality, and dishonesty".⁴⁴ A few days later, the same newspaper, the *Colonist*, carried a letter which could safely be attributed to him: Bronkhurst spoke of coolies at Bourda, where he was based, being "awful boasters . . . pretend[ing] that they can make a camel pass through a needle's eye".⁴⁵

Tyran Ramnarine, commenting on the emergence of an Indo-Guyanese tradition of letter-writing to the newspapers, "when airing their grievances", points out that the first letter was probably written in 1882 after an Indian had read in the *Colonist* newspaper that "we coolies are called liars"; his response appeared in the *Daily Chronicle*.⁴⁶ This Indian was, in fact, responding to Bronkhurst's article cited above; but he seemed to have responded, first, to the *Colonist* of 28 March 1882 where he wrote:

Sir, Having read your paper of the 27th instant [March 1882], that we coolies are called 'Liars', I beg leave to be allowed to contradict that statement, there are good and bad in all classes, by publishing this letter you will oblige
Yours truly
AGRA AND DELHIE
Lot 31, Fort Street, Kingston.

The same person, "Agra and Delhie", seems to have written the letter referred to by Ramnarine above and published in the *Daily Chronicle*, 9 May 1882. The letter is virtually the same as the one above, but the writer uses another pseudonym, a different address and adopts a transparently affected literary incompetence:

Sir, Having Read in *colonist* paper of the 22 march 1882 that we coolies are called liars, I Beg leave to be allowed to contradict that statement. There are good and bad in all classes. By publishing this letter you Will oblige,
Yours truely,

Allahabad and Benarse [*sic*]
Indian man Balesmor
tee [*sic*] many Immigrant
Mahaica, East Coast.

But Bronkhurst won the respect of educated Indo-Guyanese, like Joseph Ruhomon, with the more ennobling strand in his perception. This probably answered a deep void in the man's own psyche and sprang from delicate, submerged promptings of his Indianness. These were deeper than his impregnable Christian faith, and were shaped by his many travels away from India. He could only be an Indian to the rest of the world, where Anglo-Indian susceptibilities were nugatory and India's uncompromising caste instincts irrelevant. His formidable knowledge of ancient India enabled him to articulate a compensatory Indianness, rooted in old excellence.

Like the educated Indian elite in the nineteenth century, Bronkhurst could evoke and embrace that older India, the source of mastery in every sphere of civilized endeavour – sculpture, art, architecture, literature, and music – long antecedent to any comparable accomplishments in Europe. Civilized man in India was fashioning this excellence, he would often argue, while European man was still steeped in barbarism; and he would always claim India as his "own native home".[47] But he also claimed the formidable ancient heritage of India for the despised "coolies" of British Guiana: "Those who have read the history of India – ancient as well as modern – will admit that these people [in British Guiana], at least their forefathers, have very largely contributed towards extending our knowledge of nature in mathematics, astronomy, mechanics, and other sciences, such as arithmetic, geography, algebra, etc."[48]

Bronkhurst's splintered psyche, rooted in his ambivalent Eurasian provenance, would obtrude even in the heat of his despair with "my own countrymen, the East Indian Immigrants"[49] in British Guiana. Reflecting on their intransigence when presented with the "truth", Christianity, he noted that for the "heathen Indian . . . brought up as he is in a grovelling religion, the pure and sublime doctrines of Christianity have no attraction".[50] Yet he attributed their implacability to their awareness of their own illustrious antecedence:

[A]mongst the Immigrants there are a great many persons who are highly educated, and who have a civilisation and religion of their own to point back to, long antecedent to the days when our ancestors [Europeans] were savages covered with skins of beasts . . . The Hindo-Guyanians [Indians born in British Guiana] . . . as soon as they are born, breathe an atmosphere impregnated with Hindu doctrines . . . As you press the claims of Christ upon them, they oppose you with arguments which are not to be despised. Too frequently the cleverness and perspicuity of their reasoning, the aptness of their illustration, would put to shame many an intelligent West Indian or an English boy. The Muhammedan Indian . . . will hardly condescend to hear him. In his proud estimation, the Christian teacher can have nothing to offer him worthy of his consideration and acceptance.[51]

The Shaping of an Intellect

In exhorting young Indians in the colony to reclaim their dignity from the degradation of indentureship, to reshape a sense of honour and pride of heritage by asserting an identity with ancient Indian achievements, Bronkhurst was fortifying their security in their Hindu and Islamic legacies, thus reinforcing Indo-Guyanese resistance to his ministry. Hindus and Muslims, caught in a common servitude, could appropriate notions of India's rich, malleable past – an India of the imagination – as they challenged the assumptions of plantation society.[52] This was the positive stream, of self-affirmation, of claims to civilization, fed by Bronkhurst; and for Christian Indians like Joseph Ruhomon, also, with the "coolie" stamp of inferiority and coarseness clinging to them like barnacles, mocking their tentative progress and tenuous self-belief, this strand of Bronkhurst's thought was irresistible. In the late 1880s Bronkhurst had written, somewhat triumphantly:

[W]hy should the young man of the Colony, in whose veins runs the Indian blood, lag behind, or in any way appear to be inferior to other races in the Colony? Let us be worthy descendants of our forefathers, whose aims were far higher and more sublime, and in whose veins ran the milk of humanity, who maintained the freedom of men and women alike. If we are truly proud of being the sons of India, then let us try to be a true pride of India, the home of our ancestors, whence in bygone days enlightenment and civilization travelled to the other parts of the world.[53]

It was a clarion call; so that when, in October 1894, the young Joseph Ruhomon gave his lecture, "India; The Progress of Her People at Home and Abroad and How Those in British Guiana May Improve Themselves", amidst routine denigration of the character of "coolies", he could boldly proclaim his pride in India's past, with triumphal expectations for the future of her peoples, "at home and abroad". Ruhomon, however, was not bedevilled by the nagging ambivalence of identity of his mentor, Bronkhurst. This he proclaimed in his lecture – though he was dogged by the deflating "coolie" persona and, whether he was aware of it or not, by his Christianity with its creole assumptions of superiority, a threat to his Indian identity.

Ruhomon was, therefore, careful to assert his Indianness, while underlining his debt to "a distinguished, grand old, East Indian Christian Missionary of many years' standing [H.V.P. Bronkhurst]" (p. 13), for providing the intellectual foundations of his Indian heritage, thus enabling him to salvage his, if not his compatriots', pride from the stigma of indentureship. Ruhomon states the rationale for his path-finding lecture of 1894:

It is a common saying in this Colony that East Indians have nothing good in them; that they are an inherently lazy and vagabond class; that they are only fit to come over to this Colony as immigrants in ship loads to till the white man's field to get the white man's money and to go back to their country and live a comfortable idle life. But I hope I shall be able to dispel this erroneous impression from the minds of many tonight. East Indians are an inherently great people, and I feel supremely proud of the fact as one who has the pure, genuine East Indian blood flowing in his veins. In their own literature, science, and art, East Indians have held their own. (p. 13)

He proceeds to quote Bronkhurst, to sketch the source of the reshaping of his perceptions of self:

Indians have produced poets, philosophers, and mathematicians, such as Vyas, Gautam, Kalidas, Bhawanbhut, Bhasker, Acharya, and a host of others, whose original lofty genius is now universally admitted by those who have deeply studied them to be by no means inferior to that of Shakespeare, Locke, and Newton, making due allowance, however, for the remote age in which they flourished. (p. 28)[54]

Ruhomon was saying that his people were not "coolies" – and he never referred to Indians as "coolies". In an age when no one, neither Bronkhurst nor Bechu, later, deprecated the use of this pejorative term, this was heroic.

CHAPTER THREE

On Reading *India; The Progress Of Her People at Home and Abroad*: Some Contextual Thoughts

On Thursday, 4 October 1894, the *Daily Chronicle* carried the following terse item:

A Lecture will be delivered by Mr. J. Ruhomon, in St. Leonard's School Room [Georgetown], tonight at half-past seven o'clock, on "India; The Progress of Her People at Home and Abroad, and how those in British Guiana may improve themselves." Mr. R.D. Thomas, an East Indian, will preside.

Two days before, the same newspaper had carried the following item with the accompanying caption:

MURDER OF A COOLIE WOMAN
THE VICTIM WAS HACKED WITH A CUTLASS
JEALOUSY AND INFEDELITY

A murder betraying all the features of cold-blooded and pre-meditated ferocity, which usually characterises coolie crime, was committed yesterday morning between seven and eight o'clock, in a yard situated at Lot 202 Upper Charlotte St., Bourda. In this case the victim was a woman, and she was killed by her paramour, who without the slightest warning fell upon her as she was issuing from the passage of the yard in which she lived and literally hacked at her neck with a cutlass until she died.[55]

Indeed, in 1894, in spite of chronically poor sugar prices, 6,585 Indian indentured labourers entered British Guiana. In that year, there were still 15,858 Indian men and 6,512 Indian women under indentureship on the sugar estates, as "bound coolies".[56] This ongoing sexual imbalance had spawned rampant allegations of sexual infidelity committed by wives; it fed a culture of suspicion and violence towards women. Between 1884 and 1895, 36 of 72 murders of Indian women by indentured Indian men were attributed to "jealousy".[57] Writing on this subject in the early 1880s, H.V.P. Bronkhurst had argued:

It was well known that stoical indifference to death is a marked trait in the Coolie character: practical experience as well as books teach us this indisputable fact. Let death come, no matter with what accompaniments, to the Hindu in his deep-rooted belief, it is but a passage to an elysium – a heritage of bliss forever. The Coolie cares very little whether he is hanged or shot: in short he cares very little for the deprivation of life; and therefore he does not spare his hand in his onslaught upon human life.[58]

This was the soil which yielded myriad dark notions of the "coolie", for decades to come. Over twenty years later, in January 1904, a correspondent to the *Daily Chronicle* complained of the presence of "coolie rapscallions" [newly arrived indentured labourers from India], on the Sea Wall of Georgetown. This "observer" described them as "dirty, offensive-looking objects" who "infested" the benches where little children of the genteel, with their nurses, played in the afternoon. He added that their presence outraged "sight and smell as well as decency and sanitation", while their "peculiar manners", before impressionable children, were reprehensible. He concluded: "A respectable East Indian in his clean draperies no on could object to, but these rapscallions, and the miserable-looking women and children who follow them really should be kept in the quarters best suited to them."[59] They should be quarantined.

However, well into the 1920s and 1930s, even the "respectable East Indian", often, could not elude the resilient "coolie" image and its unsavoury associations. Incremental economic improvement, from the 1890s, had lifted the self-esteem of some. But for creole society, with its inflexible adherence to Eurocentric notions of civility and refinement, Indo-Guyanese progress with rice, cattle, and various small businesses, commonly was interpreted as evidence of their greed and meanness, another manifestation of their lack of civilized breeding.[60] Recognition did not come easily in this world of snobbery and stubborn hierarchies.

Edgar Mittelholzer (1909–1965), the Guyanese novelist from New Amsterdam, has left us a poignant tale of the resilience of the "coolie" persona in colonial society. His parents were lower middle-class coloured people; their neighbour, E.A. Luckhoo, the cousin of Joseph Ruhomon, was a distinguished civic leader and an eminent solicitor; the time would have been just after World War I. Mittelholzer recalls:

The East Indian family to the west of us had been accepted into middle-class circles, for Mr. Edward Luckhoo was a solicitor . . . But those were the days when only a very few East Indians had "emerged" from the plantation swarm of coolies – a people looked down upon socially by the whites and middle-class admixtures. So even though we were friendly with the Luckhoos – and this continued until I was fifteen or sixteen – there persisted among my aunts and my mother a continual whispering snobbism . . . My sister and I were made to feel that we could go over and play with the children, but that it must not be overdone . . . "After all, they're not really our sort", my mother might murmur. Or my aunt: "Those are people you can't trust. They're so secretive and cunning. Coolies! H'm!"[61]

India; The Progress of Her People at Home and Abroad was the first intellectual challenge by an Indo-Guyanese to the standard stereotyping. As argued earlier, the "discovery" of India was fundamental to the rise of a positive self-image, and Ruhomon uses it adroitly in his effort to initiate a "spirit of progress" among the Indians in British Guiana. He makes it clear that he is no "coolie": "I am a warm and enthusiastic lover of my race and the country of my ancestors" (p. 49). He then argues that the age is animated by "the spirit of progress": "Mankind is growing wiser, better, and more enlightened under the purifying influence of civilization. There is no more that intellectual and moral torpor or stagnation which existed in the centuries gone by" (p. 49). He applauds the phenomenal achievements by Europeans in literature, science and philosophy, having "beaten back and eclipsed" all previous efforts (p. 49).

Ruhomon observes, however, that this "spirit of progress" was being disseminated in Africa and India, where progressive European influences have been absorbed and have fired the imagination of a new generation of Africans and Indians, who were conquering ignorance and obscurantism, with knowledge, as they tried to reclaim their ancient greatness (pp. 49–64). It was characteristic of Ruhomon that he was not enamoured of racist rhetoric, never paraded a chauvinistic nationalism, and was careful not to hurt the sensibilities of his African Guyanese compatriots. In an age when it was axiomatic to denigrate Africa and India, he celebrated the eminence of both Africans and Indians:

Two of the greatest nations in the world that have been noted for gross moral and intellectual darkness were Africans and East Indians. Both were renowned many, many centuries ago. Both have had an interrupted career, both have had a break in the course of their progress . . . and both today are climbing up the ladder of progress. (p. 53)

Ruhomon observes: "The negroes are a great people; they have been so from the earliest times, and though there have been many impediments to their progress, they are rising and making their influence felt far and wide . . . Africans have been famous from the earliest times" (p. 52). The contemporary achievements of several people of African descent are noted (pp. 51–53), and his magnanimity and respect for them in British Guiana are underlined:

Here, intellectually, morally, religiously and socially, they are wonderfully improving, in spite of numerous difficulties and discouragements and obstacles in their way, and the abominable and much-to-be-deplored racial prejudice which is so firmly rooted in the community. (p. 65)

He was especially impressed with what he saw as the rising intellectual stature of his African Guyanese compatriots, and commended the sacrifices which some black parents were making to give their children a sound primary and secondary education, even professional education overseas. The African man, having lifted himself from the despair of slavery, Ruhomon concluded, "[n]othing can now contort or cripple the giant might of his nature and hinder him in his march of progress" (p. 65).

Ruhomon was deeply pained, however, by what he saw as the sad, static position of the Indo-Guyanese people, in the 1890s. He argued: "We have done nothing in the Colony that has resounded to our credit . . .The poorer classes of people are simply 'no-bodies' in the community . . . The East Indian race in British Guiana has not yet begun its history as a race. Its past has been chaos and darkness" (pp. 66–68).

This bleak assessment, of course, is only partially correct, but it does underline Ruhomon's belief that his Indian compatriots had much to learn from the African Guyanese people. As a man who had discovered the fount of Western scholarship, the breath of knowledge spawned by the spirit of inquiry cultivated within the European intellectual tradition, he was impatient with what he considered a fetish for narrow materialism among Indians in British Guiana. It was his fascination with Western scholarship on India, its extolling of diverse strands of the latter's ancient grandeur, which had inspired in him confidence in the "genius, intelligence, and industry" of the Indian people (p. 60).

Ruhomon believed that the people of India "will be able to live independently of British rule, will have the powers of Government thrust into their own hands, and will know how to look after their own affairs". His conviction was based on his assessment that in many professions – medicine, law, politics, journalism – Indians "have proved themselves to be equal in ability, if not superior, to their fair-faced brothers". He continued: "They have, indeed, drunk deep draughts at the fountain of European thought and learning, and there is no question about them being beaten in competition with Europeans." This could have been an allusion to Joseph Ruhomon's own growing self-belief (p. 60).

By the 1890s the achievements of several Indians overseas also impressed him: university students in Britain, especially the entry of a few Indian women studying medicine (p. 61); the election of Dadabhai Naoroji to the House of Commons in 1892 (pp. 61–62); the elevation of Hafiz Abdul Karim as minister and Indian secretary to Queen Victoria (p. 61); the brilliant oratorical expositions of Swami Vivekananda at the World's Parliament of Religions in Chicago, in September 1893 (p. 63). These were some of the solid gains of Indian intellect which provided the foundation of his own self-belief; they also nourished his hopes for, and quickened his frustration with, his Indo-Guyanese people. Repelled and agitated by the resilient "coolie" shadow, he championed what became virtually a doctrine: the development of the intellect; "the polish of mind and character". Ruhomon was committed to the education of boys *and* girls, wide reading, and the creation of organizations for young men *and* young women for their "intellectual, moral, and social" development (pp. 68–70).

Throughout his life, Joseph Ruhomon was free of narrow racial or sexist prejudices. He saw women as "one of the most powerful . . . forces at work in this 19th century, not only for the emancipation of her sex but in the common cause of humanity". And he challenged Indo-Guyanese men to encourage the education of their women and their participation in community affairs; because "in association with our young women . . . you will obtain far better results in seeking to advance your own interests and the interests of our people than you can by working alone" (p. 70). Over one hundred years later, this message has not lost its poignancy or its relevance.

However, the young man's rather bleak assessment of the Indo-Guyanese condition, in the 1890s, overlooked many small but important achievements by his people. Of course, as a Christian Indian, in the context of his time, it was difficult for him to see that the resolute adherence of Hindus and Muslims to their ancestral creeds constituted a culture of resistance, fed by their own ancient reverences, epic tales of revolt and legendary heroes. This tradition of cultural resilience was itself heroic, as Christian missionary work among the Indians intensified from the 1860s. In 1877 a pamphleteer in British Guiana had reflected on the resilience of the "Hindoos and Mohometans [sic]", but he saw this as a defect, as was the fashion:

The strangers obstinately adhered to their own religion, except when, here and there, a designing fellow, for some mercenary object, consented to be baptised, and brought discredit on Christianity by his unprincipled conduct; until "Christian Coolie" became a by-word for everything that was base, villainous, and disreputable.[62]

The Indians in British Guiana had, indeed, begun their history. Joseph Ruhomon's youthful impatience notwithstanding, he was too near to the world of the "coolie" and its inhibiting taint to be dispassionate, but there were, before the 1890s, innumerable acts of individual and collective resistance practised on the sugar plantations. In fact, the racial arrogance and arbitrary conduct of many white overseers and their wanton projection of power, which often led to the seduction of Indian women in the fields, bred what seemed like a tradition of "overseer beating" among Indian male labourers. As a local correspondent wrote evocatively in June 1893: "It looks as if the season for overseer beating had set in, and the coolies were determined to have some good sport of it."[63]

Throughout indentureship, but especially after riots at Plantation Leonora in 1869, there were numerous cases of collective action by Indo-Guyanese men and women in an age when the sanctions were severe. No established mechanisms existed for the ventilation of grievances beyond attracting the attention of the immigration agent general or his agent by some dramatic action.[64] In 1872, when Indian workers at Devonshire Castle (Essequibo) protested, five were killed; later, in 1896, five more protesting workers were killed at Non Pareil (East Coast Demerara). Between 1886 and 1889 there were at least one hundred strikes (forty-two in 1888), initiated by Indian workers on the plantations. In 1894, the year of Ruhomon's path-finding lecture, there were "principal disturbances" at Leguan, Farm, Success, Skeldon, and La Bonne Mere estates.[65] This, also, is an aspect of the Indo-Guyanese achievement; but it was episodic. There were also the daily, unspectacular, individual fight for dignity, thus affirming the humanity and integrity of the protestors. Their history had already begun.

Ruhomon had exhorted his compatriots to be "bold, strong, fearless, acquitting themselves like men", as they struggled to advance (p. 67). There were many illiterate "coolies", on the sugar estates, who were already doing so. But, by the late 1890s, as Tyran Ramnarine has brought to our attention, there was a unique resister, a bound "coolie" radical at Plantation Enmore, Bechu – a man of intellect, wit and exemplary courage. Bechu was challenging the plantocracy in numerous letters to the *Daily Chronicle*, exposing one oppressive practice or another.[66] In his first letter to the *Daily Chronicle* (1 November 1896), following the shooting of Indian labourers at Non Pareil on 13 October, he asserted:

In this Colony . . . an argument appears to be binding on one side only, for we constantly see coolies being brought up for "neglecting to attend work", for "not completing their task", and for many such trivial breaches of contract, but in not a single instance have I seen a "Protector" [the Immigration Agent] charge an employer for not fulfilling his part of the contract towards an indentured immigrant. Is this fair play?

Bechu showed amazing fortitude when he appeared before the West India Royal Commission of 1897, the first Indo-Guyanese to do so. Although still a "bound coolie" at Enmore, he deprecated the conduct of the immigration agent of his district in his memorandum to the commission: "Besides taking no interest in the coolies, whose protector he is supposed to be, he is on such friendly terms with the manager as to have succeeded in getting his daughter employment in his house as governess. How is it possible, under the circumstance, to receive justice at his hands?"[67]

This culture of resistance, of self-affirmation, was rooted in discernible economic achievements. From the 1890s, as sugar faced continued depression, the Government of British Guiana gradually began to ease the draconian terms of Crown Lands acquisition. Minor constitutional changes, also, were introduced in 1891. Many Indians were beneficiaries of these liberal measures. Along the coastland, often in the vicinity of their old plantations as well as along the lower reaches of the rivers, an energetic land-owning, agricultural population was emerging. This enabled many to be independent of plantation labour, to experiment further with rice cultivation, cattle-rearing, fruits and vegetables – activities which had been initiated on the sugar estates during indentureship. These enterprises were the catalyst for the rise of rural entrepreneurship – rice milling, cattle rearing and shopkeeping in the villages and on the estates.[68]

Already, by 1894, about 7,500 acres were under rice cultivation. The immigration agent general, in his report for 1896–97, observed: "[T]here can be no doubt that this Colony is particularly suitable for rice-growing and as each year witnesses a further development of it, there is some reason to look forward to its being a valuable industry, and to its affording remunerative occupation to large numbers of the East Indian population."[69] This was prophetic. Between 1899 and 1903, about 15,000 acres per year were under rice cultivation; World War I stimulated a phenomenal increase, reaching about 60,000 acres by 1918. In 1908–9 rice exports were valued at $240,000; by 1916, $1,044,000.[70]

In 1891 D.W.D. Comins, the protector of immigrants (Calcutta), was on an official visit to British Guiana (and other colonies), to assess the condition of Indians. On 16 August he travelled between Lots 63 and 75, on the Upper Corentyne Coast, Berbice, and was deeply satisfied with the diversity of their agricultural pursuits and a perceptible self-assurance shaped by economic security. Comins observed:

All the coolies' houses are built along the front of these lots, facing the road ... Their land lies at the back and is planted in rice, corn, plantains, and cassava. The front land is planted with cocoanut [sic] trees, and a plot is reserved round the house for mango, guava and other fruit trees, which also afford shade for their cattle, fowls, donkeys, goats etc., of which they have a great number. Many of the houses have a cattle shed or pen near the house, in which calves and young cattle are kept. In front of many of the houses I saw rice drying, and in some they were pounding rice with "dhenkies". One cannot help being struck by the great happiness and contentment of the women and children in their self-chosen homes. The children are fat, sturdy, and well-groomed, and the mothers well-dressed and smiling. In one place a vigorous game of cricket was going on among cooly [sic] boys. Nearly every house had a donkey cart, in which owners either go themselves or carry fruit, vegetables, grain, etc., to market ... It is difficult to recognise in these happy, contented, prosperous, and worldly-wise people, living comfortably and independently on their own property, and rapidly acquiring wealth and importance of position as thriving settlers, the ignorant, penniless, bigoted, and intensely stupid coolies who left Calcutta only a few years previously.[71]

This condition of seminal achievement and contentment did not obtain everywhere, in all villages and plantations, but it pointed to possibilities for advancement, and inspired others to beat back the barriers – psychological and material – rooted in the "coolie" universe of limitations. The 1890s were a watershed in Indo-Guyanese history. A few central personalities began to people accounts of their experience – recognized exemplars of individual initiative and progress, solid anchors for dreams of a fuller life beyond the sugar estates.

One such figure was Edun (1822–1904), the head driver at Plantation Philadelphia, West Coast Demerara. Comins visited him in July 1891, and reported:

Edun has a cattle farm and provision ground called Khamarai, which he values at $15,000; there are 1,875 acres, and it is freehold property ... much of it is well-cultivated in plantains, cassava, and Indian-corn and okras. Some of it is still in forest, and he is cutting cord wood. He also grows yams, castor-oil, cocoanuts [sic], and tanias.[72]

Edun had gone to British Guiana as an indentured labourer in the early 1850s, in the ship *Soubadhar*. He worked himself to the position of "head driver" and subsequently bought Orangestein, the estate Comins visited. When Edun died in March 1904, aged eighty-two, it was noted that he was held in high esteem by several managers with whom he had worked on the plantation; moreover, it was a measure of his stature among his Indian compatriots that "whenever there was any dissatisfaction about the price of wages paid for work, Edun was invariably selected as one of the arbitrators".[73] He was survived by his widow, three children, and twenty-five grandchildren. One of his sons, Noor Mohamed Edun, had worked in the Immigration Office before becoming a Hindi interpreter in the Magistrate's Court on the West Coast Demerara. In 1937 Edun's grandson Ayube Edun (born 1893), founded the first trade union for plantation workers.

So it would seem as if astounding material progress did not lead to a severing of links with the roots of the family's achievement; it definitely did not diminish the respect which Edun's African and Indian compatriots retained for him. His funeral, in March 1904, was considered "one of the largest ever seen on the Coast. Mussalmans [Muslims] and Hindoos, besides over two hundred black people, followed in the procession."[74] As usual, nothing was said of the man's wife. She, too, must have been a person of considerable strength, initiative and consistency of purpose. Edun's life belongs to the history of embryonic effort and achievement of the Indo-Guyanese people; but it was not the sort of example that would have readily impressed the young Joseph Ruhomon.[75]

In 1891 Comins had struck at the core of the new Indian persona which was taking shape on the sugar plantations; it was reflected in a growing ease, a perceptible self-assurance, children being at ease in the presence of white men:

I have been much struck, on my visits to many of the estates . . . with the trust and affection shown by the coolies, especially the children, to the manager. The ordinary small child in India, at the sight of a sahib [white man] coming into the place, would howl and fly in precipitate dismay; but here they have complete confidence in him, and crowd round delighted and beaming at any small attention they receive . . .[76]

He elaborated, relating a tale of discernible cockiness from Plantation Port Mourant, on the lower Corentyne Coast, in Berbice. As noted earlier, Joseph Ruhomon's father had worked on this progressive estate, in a healthy, less malarial district. Most Indian labourers here were given land to grow rice and rear cattle.[77] Material progress spawned an independence of spirit, which found expression in a fanatical attachment to cricket, already the premier game in the colony. Comins was at Port Mourant on 15 August 1891; the incident is from the previous month:

Fifteen or sixteen colony-born cooly [sic] youths (Creoles) asked for a three days' pass to plant rice on their own lands. Instead of doing this they went to cricket matches for three days, and then were absent for three more days on their own ground. Mr. Murray [the Manager] summoned them, and they were fined $3 or seven days in jail, which latter alternative they all preferred. These were some of his best shovelmen, born on the estate, and in receipt of high wages, and all took money with them to pay their fines, but when they heard their stay in jail was to be so short, they all decided to go to jail.[78]

This is the sugar plantation that produced John Trim, Rohan Kanhai, Basil Butcher, Joe Solomon, Ivan Madray, and Alvin Kallicharran – West Indian Test cricketers; another Test cricketer, Roy Fredericks, came from another Berbice plantation, Blairmont. This astounding achievement in sports was shaped by life and labour on the sugar estates.[79]

Proficiency at cricket was a potent symbol of arrival in creole society. The game was encouraged by managers on the estates, possibly as an instrument for canalizing youthful energy, and stemming disaffection and susceptibility to "agitators". Indo-Guyanese youths embraced cricket with a passion. This helped, immeasurably, to build a delicate tolerance – the rudiments of an understanding across the racial divide, between Africans and Indians. As Comins reported in 1891:

Many of the sons of East Indians born in the colony play cricket regularly. On Saturday afternoon on most estates a game can be seen going on, the players being partly Creole cooly [sic] boys and partly black, and the game is played with great spirit. Many managers encourage them to play, and some even get up rival matches with neighbouring estates.[80]

By 1895, in Georgetown, a few middle-class Indian men had acquired the self-confidence to form the first organized Indo-Guyanese cricket club, the Asiatic Cricket Club. On 26 December 1895, they played their maiden match against a Portuguese team, the Lusitana Cricket Club, at the Militia Parade Ground, Georgetown.[81] Asiatic won by thirty-eight runs and the captain, F.E. Jaundoo, was commended "for the able manner in which he conducted the game throughout".[82] Asiatic was the forerunner of the celebrated British Guiana East Indian Cricket Club, founded in Georgetown in 1914 by J.A. Veerasawmy, a lawyer, the first Indian to represent British Guiana in inter-colonial cricket, in 1910.[83]

This seemingly minor victory, in December 1895, was an historic achievement: it was gained against the Portuguese, the ascendant group in

1890s' British Guiana, with an equally avid commitment to the game; the team comprised Hindu, Muslim, and Christian Indians, of north Indian as well as Tamil ancestry – a distinguished feature of Indo-Guyanese cricket since. To play cricket in the British West Indies was to begin to stake an emphatic claim for recognition in creole society; to possess something of the spirit of the place; to be of it. It is noteworthy that this elevation in the stature of Indo-Guyanese cricket coincided with the meteoric rise in England of the great Indian cricketer, Prince Ranjitsinhji (1872–1933). From the mid-1890s on, his elegant stroke-play, his "lightning quickness of conception and execution", enthralled all: those who saw him; those who read of him; even those, like many illiterate Indo-Guyanese coolies, who could only imagine the mastery.[84]

Indo-Guyanese history had already begun: their pride in the Prince of cricket "the finest exponent of the game",[85] their own competence in the game and elevation to organized cricket in Georgetown were congruent with the spirit of the place. Joseph Ruhomon might not have noticed this; he was calling for the lifting of their intellectual imagination, the founding of societies to promote their self-interest. This, also, had begun by the 1890s, however faltering or spasmodic. The founding of the short-lived British Guiana East Indian Institute in 1892,[86] possibly the first Indian organization in the Caribbean, marked the start of the quest for self-expression. Its principal members were James Wharton and his brother William Hewley Wharton, F.E. Jaundoo, the cricketer, Thomas Flood, the businessman and, later, first president of the East Indian Cricket Club, and Veerasawmy Mudaliar, former chief interpreter of the Immigration Department and father of the cricketer, J.A. Veerasawmy.

One of the reasons for the sudden death of the East Indian Institute was the departure, in mid-1893, of William Hewley Wharton for the University of Edinburgh. He was the first Indian in the Caribbean to study at a British university. An outstanding student, he won recognition from his colleagues from India, being elected secretary of the prestigious Edinburgh Indian Association in 1896 and president in 1898–99. Wharton's graduation as a doctor of medicine, in 1899, was a watershed in Indo-Caribbean professional history,[87] and some of his compatriots in British Guiana celebrated this monumental achievement, in December of that year:

An interesting function took place on Thursday evening at the residence of Mr. Thomas Flood, Bourda. It took the shape of a presentation of an appropriately worded address of welcome to Dr. W. Hewley Wharton from some of the leading East Indian citizens, including Messrs Goolmohamed Khan, [Thomas] Flood, F.E. Jaundoo, Veerasawmy [Mudaliar], Soobrian, Goolamally, etc. The presentation was made by Mr. Jaundoo, Chief East Indian interpreter. In the address, expression was given to the donors' pride of welcoming the first East Indian native of the Colony as a doctor, and reference was made to Dr. Wharton's brilliant career and his valuable discoveries in his profession. The doctor suitably replied. Afterwards refreshments were served, and a pleasant evening was made still more enjoyable by the playing of a select programme of music by the Misses Flood.[88]

Significantly, E.A. Luckhoo, the first Indian solicitor in British Guiana and a cousin of Joseph Ruhomon, had started his practice in New Amsterdam a few months before, in September 1899.[89] The "coolie" was, indeed, beginning to demand recognition. Although these were the individual achievements of two young men, they were massive, seminal psychological feats belonging to all Indo-Guyanese. An intellectual tradition was being established.

During the Indian Centenary celebrations in 1938, nearly forty-four years after his 1894 lecture, Joseph Ruhomon was able to acknowledge the intellectual progress of his compatriots. He observed:

Cases of signal educational advancement among individual Indians are many; and this has only proved the native capacity of the race for mental culture, and such has provided the basis for intellectual triumphs in varied fields, for success in professional and business life, for representative duties in the Legislature and on public boards . . . As regards the social and religious features of Indian life, they are to be seen in the activities of various institutions or organizations – among these being the B.G.E.I. Association, the "Susamachar" [Wesleyan] Young Men's Society, the Indian Literary Society . . . , the Hindu Religious Society . . . , the American Aryan League, the Balak Sahaita Mandalee, the Islamic Association, the BG Dramatic Society, the B.G.E.I. Cricket Club, the Corentyne Literary and Debating Society, the Canadian E.I. Mission, and the Salvation Army.[90]

In Joseph Ruhomon's lifetime, a solid record of study, academic brilliance, and professional excellence had already cohered, guiding many beyond the limitations of the plantations and the shame of the "coolie" stain. But these accomplishments could not have been realized without the thrift, continuity of purpose and enduring commitment to family, reflected in unremitting, arduous work in the rice fields, cattle pastures, sugar estates, and provision and dry goods shops, by men, women, and children on the malarial coastland of British Guiana. This is, indeed, a history of achievement and Joseph Ruhomon did much to shape it.

It is now over a hundred years since Joseph Ruhomon's *India; The Progress of Her People at Home and Abroad, and How Those in British Guiana May Improve Themselves* appeared; but Peter Ruhomon's tribute to his brother shortly after his death in 1942 remains unassailable:

AU REVOIR!
(A Brother's Tribute to the Late Joseph Ruhomon)

Unheralded,
As flash precedes the thunder-clap,
Or smoke reveals the hidden fire;
But softly, as the fall of night,
Into the silent deep he passed.

His was a life,
Attuned to higher, nobler things.
Within the dank and fet'd breath
O' Earth's decaying life, he caught
The rhythm of a sweeter strain.

And in the web of Cosmic life,
A moral purpose grand he read;
And with this high design he
– wrought
to bring his life in right accord.

With warm Hebraic zeal,
He fought the cause of human
– rights;
Acclaiming what is good and just;
Condemning what appeareth
– wrong.

To light the path of those who
– sought,
To understand he held aloft
The torch of Truth as best he knew,
Guiding, instructing, counselling,

On Reading *India*

That all may reach the Better Land
Where darkness broodeth not and
– Life
In all its fullness stands revealed.[91]

NOTES TO PART 1

1. See my *India and the Shaping of the Indo-Guyanese Imagination, 1890s–1920s* (Leeds: Peepal Tree Books/University of Warwick, 1993), part 2, "Joseph Ruhomon and his 'Discovery' of India, 1894", 18–28.
2. As late as March 1920, Mungal Singh, an Indo-Guyanese lawyer, was bemoaning the insult occasioned by the use of the "opprobrious" term, "coolie". It was "flashed and dashed about indiscriminately . . . flaunted in the faces of ladies and gentlemen". *Daily Argosy*, 27 March 1920.
3. In 1891 only 5.8 percent of "professional (including Public Service)" jobs were held by Indians; in 1911, this had increased marginally to 8.2 percent (Dwarka Nath, *A History of Indians in Guyana* [London: The Author, 1970 {1950}], 241). Tyran Ramnarine unveils the reality behind these bald figures: in 1912, of 596 Indo-Guyanese employed in the civil service, 448 were "messengers, porters, gardeners, or day labourers". He adds: "Throughout the period of indenture, Indian police constables averaged less than 20 in a force of about 700. At no time did any of them serve in a rank higher than constable" (Tyran Ramnarine, "The Growth of the East Indian Community in British Guiana, 1880–1920" [Ph.D. diss., University of Sussex, 1977], 105). There were nine Indian teachers in the colony in 1891; all were men (*Census Report of British Guiana, 1891*).
4. No attempt has, hitherto, been made to assess the significance of this lecture/pamphlet to Indo-Guyanese history, although there have been some allusions to its importance. Peter Ruhomon recalled that Joseph Ruhomon's lament on the absence of an Indian organization "devoted to their moral, social and intellectual improvement" was a major prompting behind Revd H.M. Yates's initiative in forming the [Wesleyan] East Indian Young Men's Society, in 1919, in Georgetown (*Centenary History of the East Indians in British Guiana, 1838–1938* [Georgetown: East Indians 150th Anniversary Committee, 1988 {1947}], 217–18). A successor to Revd Yates as Wesleyan Missionary to the Indians and President of the East Indian Young Men's Society, Revd H.H. Chick, observed, in November 1934, of Joseph Ruhomon's 1894 lecture/pamphlet that it "was saddened by a pitiful lament over the backward condition of the East Indian Community". He, also, noted that Ruhomon concluded "with an eloquent appeal to his fellow-countrymen to form themselves into societies devoted to the intellectual, moral and social improvement of its members" (Foreword to *Anthology of Local Indian Verse*, ed. C.E.J. Ramcharitar-Lalla [Georgetown: Argosy Co., 1934], 7).
5. I have relied heavily on the following sources for the compilation of this biographical sketch of the Ruhomons and the Luckhoos: Nath, *A History of the Indians in Guyana*, 201–3; *Who Is Who in British Guiana, 1935–1937* (Georgetown: Daily Chronicle Ltd, 1937); *Who Is Who in British Guiana, 1945–1948* (Georgetown: Daily Chronicle Ltd, 1948).
6. *Daily Argosy*, 25 November 1921, carried the following terse report from Berbice: "The death of Mr. Pahalad took place at Rose Hall, Corentyne, a few days ago.

Mr. Pahalad was a brother of the late Mr. Moses Luckhoo and Mr. John Ruhomon."

7. *The Census Report of British Guiana, 1891*, recorded twenty-one chemists and druggists who were Indians. For a few this competence, acquired on the sugar plantations, was identified early as an avenue of mobility.

8. Edward Alfred Luckhoo was admitted to practise as a solicitor on 8 September 1899; he was presented with a congratulatory address on the following day (*Berbice Gazette*, 3 January 1900).

9. Joseph Alexander Luckhoo (1887–1949) had worked in his father's firm after he left Queen's College. He studied law in London at the Middle Temple between 1909 and 1912. He returned to British Guiana in September 1912 and proceeded to build a formidable legal reputation. In October 1916, he was the first Indo-Guyanese to be elected to the local legislature. In 1923, at the age of thirty-six, he was made a king's counsel, the first Indian outside India to achieve that distinction (*Daily Argosy*, 7 October 1923).

10. "Indian Intelligence by the Pundit" [Peter Ruhomon], *Daily Chronicle* (magazine section), 13 July 1930; Nath, *History of Indians in Guyana*, 202.

11. In June 1916 a brilliant young doctor, a graduate in Tropical Medicine and Bacteriology from Edinburgh and the London School of Tropical Medicine, Dr Loris Rohan Sharples, applied for the post of government medical officer (GMO). He was from a distinguished coloured family, and had acted as assistant GMO at the Georgetown Hospital since January 1914. The surgeon general, Dr K.S. Wise, recommended him for the post, as he had "proved himself efficient and reliable". The acting governor, Cecil Clementi, wrote confidentially to the Colonial Office counselling against the appointment; his arguments reeked of racism: "I venture to remind you of the correspondence which took place between Sir Walter Edgerton [the governor] and yourself concerning the undesirability of appointing gentlemen who are not of British race to these appointments. Dr. Sharples is of mixed race (African and European). I have every reason to believe him to be an efficient medical practitioner, and to be qualified for the post for which he is now recommended, but I entirely agree with the view taken by Sir Walter Egerton that it is most undesirable, if it can be avoided, to appoint other than white doctors to the medical staff of the Colony. In out-districts to which GMO's have frequently to be assigned, they have to attend on European as well as all other classes of patients, and European residents in such districts resent the necessity of having to call in a doctor who is not of their own race." Gilbert Grindle, the Colonial Office official, minuted the secretary of state for the colonies, Bonar Law, thus: "Of course, white doctors are preferable, if they can be got, but we have several coloured doctors now, and shall have more in the future. They are better than no doctor at all – and some of them are quite good." Dr Sharples was excellent. He practised, privately, for many years in British Guiana. His work was legendary, and at Plantation Port Mourant, his main district, he became a hero of the Indian plantation workers. The great Indo-Guyanese cricketer, Rohan Kanhai (born 1935),

was named after him. (Colonial Office [CO] 111/606, Clementi to Bonar Law, no. 242, 15 July 1916; CO 111/606, confidential, 15 July 1916; Cheddi Jagan, *The West on Trial: My Struggle for Guyana's Freedom* [London: Michael Joseph, 1966], 128.)

12. Walter Rodney has written perceptively on this phenomenon among Africans and coloureds: "To complete primary school was a major achievement. The individual in this category was qualified to become a pupil teacher and to proceed upward through "certificated" grades. When young scholars completed this phase, they were immediately appointed headmasters of primary schools. Such an appointment lifted the individual out of the working class. The position of headmaster of a primary school must be viewed as constituting the cornerstone of the black and brown middle class. Biographical data on a number of prominent lawyers show that they filled the posts of headmaster as the first step in a professional career. A.B. Brown, Samuel E. Wills, McLean Ogle and many others were all young headmasters before they left the country to study law in Britain" (Walter Rodney, *A History of the Guyanese Working People, 1881–1905* [Baltimore: Johns Hopkins University Press, 1981], 115).

13. In 1934, forty years after the publication of *India; The Progress of Her People at Home and Abroad*, Revd H.H. Chick could remark, still, on the unflickering idealism and purity of motives of Joseph Ruhomon: "No one can accuse Mr. Ruhoman [sic] of losing the lofty ideals of his youth. Throughout the years, in season and out, he has steadily striven to realise the best he has known, in the lives of his friends. Recent years have witnessed a marked improvement in the people who came originally as indentured labourers from India. There are many men who have risen from very lowly positions occupying high positions in social, legal, political and business life" ("Foreword" to *Anthology of Local Indian Verse*, ed. Ramcharitar-Lalla, 7). Ruhomon's youthful exhortations of 1894 had *not* fallen on stony ground.

14. *Daily Argosy*, 16 March 1924; *Daily Chronicle*, 3 April 1924.

15. Joseph Ruhoman [sic], "The Creole East Indian", *Timehri*, 3rd ser., 7 (1921): 104.

16. Jock Campbell writes: "In 1934 I went out to work for my family's sugar business in British Guiana . . . The conditions in which past members of my family had pursued profits and made considerable fortunes came as a great shock to me. Conditions of employment were disgraceful; wages were abysmally low; housing was unspeakable; workers were treated with contempt – as chattels. Animals and machinery were, in fact, cared for better than workers because they cost money to buy and replace" (Jock Campbell, "Private Enterprise and Public Morality", *New Statesman*, 27 May 1966).

17. D.W.D. Comins, *Note on Emigration from India to British Guiana*, Diary (Calcutta: Bengal Secretariat Press, 1893), 31.

18. See my "*Tiger in the Stars*": *The Anatomy of Indian Achievement in British Guiana, 1919–29* (London: Macmillan, 1997).

19. By 1891, 294 Indian men and 38 Indian women were returned as "overseers";

these were, in fact, "drivers" or gang-leaders on the estates. They were above the mass of labourers – symbols of mobility. Joseph Ruhomon's father, occupying senior positions in several estate hospitals, would have ranked above the "drivers" (*Census Report of British Guiana, 1891*).

20. Tyran Ramnarine cites the case of an Indian correspondent to the *Argosy,* 13 June 1906, deprecating the blanket application of the pejorative term, "coolie" to all "East Indians". He wrote: "[To] once more take exception to all my fellow colonists of East Indian race and descendants being described as coolies . . . Coolies are labourers such as work on sugar estates or do odd jobs, and you will find East Indians in positions other than these. See how farmers work planting rice, and clearing and making paddy into rice. If there is ever to be any opening up of the country it is to the East Indian you must look, as he is gradually occupying the available lands for farming" (Quoted in Tyran Ramnarine, "Growth of East Indian Community in British Guiana", 219).

    This correspondent, apparently, was A.S. Khan from Richmond, Essequibo, who, a few weeks before, had observed that one writer had stated that planters would have to rely upon the "coolie" vote in the future. He countered: "[I]t is not plain what is meant by this, as there are white, black, coloured and brown coolies, but admitting in his ignorance he means East Indians", he continued, underlining his disgust at the opprobrious term (*Argosy*, 26 May 1906).

21. *Daily Argosy*, 26 September 1942.
22. Rodney, *History of the Guyanese Working People*, 177.
23. Joseph Ruhomon, *India; The Progress of Her People at Home and Abroad, and How Those in British Guiana may Improve Themselves* (Georgetown: C.K. Jardine, 1894). All references to this publication appear parenthetically in the text and page numbers are based on its reproduction in part 2 of this book.
24. See note 1. Joseph Ruhomon attended the meeting of the Berbice Library Committee in January 1894, when "a vote of thanks was passed to the Officers of the Committee and Trustees, on the motion of Mr. J. RUHOMON" (*Berbice Gazette*, 27 January 1894). It was common in New Amsterdam for departing missionaries, planters, and officials to dispose of their books by auction. Ruhomon, always hungry for good books, was probably a regular purchaser. One such auction, in March 1894, was advertised thus:

AUCTION SALE OF
VALUABLE BOOKS
The undersigned has received instructions
from
J.J. FARMER, Esq.
to expose for Sale at Public Auction
On Saturday, 31st Inst., at
Sharp 12 o'clock, noon
A LOT OF

STANDARD PUBLICATIONS
comprising
The BEST EDITIONS of all the FAMOUS AUTHORS
of Europe and America . . . .
WORKS ON SCIENCE, ART
AND LITERATURE
at LOT 15, STRAND [NEW AMSTERDAM]

D.W.A. McKinnon
(Auctioneer) — *The Berbice Gazette*,
31 March 1894

25. Rodney, *History of the Guyanese Working People*, 171–73, 177.
26. The article was reproduced in the *Argosy*, 24 November 1900, which dubbed Shirley a "tempestuous agitator", endeavouring "to set . . . the Berbice River on fire".
27. Joseph Ruhomon, "Reflections on the Season", *Berbice Gazette*, 25 December 1901.
28. *Who Is Who in British Guiana, 1935–1937; Daily Chronicle*, 5 May 1938; *Daily Chronicle*, 23 September 1942; *Daily Argosy*, 26 September 1942; Tyran Ramnarine, "East Indian Political Representation in British Guiana During the Latter Part of Indenture, 1890–1917", *Guyana Historical Journal* 2 (1990): 43.
29. *Daily Chronicle*, 23 September 1942.
30. By 1921 Ruhomon's euphoria of 1918, his dream of a "Golden Age, when armaments shall be no more, and only the arts of Peace shall be pursued" had evaporated. He foresaw a greater catastrophe: "It is thought in certain quarters that the defeated Germany is now quite impotent, that the great beast, having had its teeth drawn and its claws pared, is now incapable of doing serious mischief. We have it on high authority that Germany is unshakably bent on a terrible war of revenge. . . The nations of Europe . . . will assuredly once more and finally be drawn into another general world-embroilment leading straight to Armageddon." See his poem, "The Golden Age", in *Anthology of Local Indian Verse*, ed. Ramcharitar-Lalla, 10–13, and his *Signs and Portents: A Study of World Conditions and Prospects in the Light of Bible Prophecy* (New Amsterdam: Berbice Gazette Printing Press, 1921), 8–9, 10.
31. *Daily Argosy*, 14 July 1922.
32. *Daily Chronicle*, 18 July 1895. The paper noted that Bronkhurst "has done much for the uplifting" of East Indians, adding that he was "a man of considerable learning and ability". He was buried at La Repentir Cemetery, Georgetown.
33. Joseph Ruhomon (New Amsterdam, 18 July 1895) to the Editor, *Daily Chronicle*, 21 July 1895.
34. This biographical sketch of Bronkhurst is based on an obituary in the *Wesleyan Methodist Monthly Greeting* (July 1895), reproduced in the *Daily Chronicle*, 15 July

1895.
35. Peter Ruhomon, *Centenary History*, 213–14.
36. H.V.P. Bronkhurst was a most prolific contributor to the vibrant local press of the 1880s and early 1890s. He was the author of the following books – priceless sources of Guyanese historiography: *The Origin of the Guyanian Indians . . .* (Georgetown, Demerara: Colonist Press, 1881); *The Colony of British Guyana and its Labouring Population* (London: J. Woolmer, 1883); *The Ancestry or Origin of our East Indian Immigrants; being an Ethnological and Philological Paper* (Georgetown: Argosy Press, 1886); *Among the Hindus and Creoles of British Guyana* [sic] (London: J. Woolmer, 1888); *A Descriptive and Historical Geography of British Guiana and West India Islands* (Georgetown: Argosy Press, 1890). He also published several pamphlets on theological matters.
37. Bronkhurst, *Colony of British Guyana*, 459–60.
38. Ibid., 34–36.
39. *The Census Report of British Guiana, 1931.*
40. Ibid.
41. See note 1.
42. Bronkhurst, *Among the Hindus and Creoles*, 58.
43. For a recent study which may help to illuminate the sources of Bronkhurst's ambivalence, see Noel P. Gist and Roy Dean Wright, *Marginality and Identity: Anglo-Indians as a Racially-Mixed Minority in India* (London: E.J. Brill, 1973).
44. *Colonist*, 22 March 1882. The second and third instalments of this article appeared on 8 April and 13 April respectively. It was included in chapter 12 of Bronkhurst's *Colony of British Guyana*.
45. *Colonist*, 27 March 1882. See the *Colonist*, 18 July 1882, where Bronkhurst speaks of his missionary work among Indians at Bourda and Lacytown, "coolie town".
46. Ramnarine, "East Indian Political Representation", 38.
47. Bronkhurst, *Among the Hindus and Creoles*, 34. He wrote: "The children born and brought up in the Colony need not be ashamed of their ancestral home."
48. Bronkhurst, *Colony of British Guyana*, 238–39.
49. Bronkhurst, *Among the Hindus and Creoles*, 306.
50. Ibid., 52.
51. Ibid., 52–53.
52. For a study of the deep-seated, redemptive impact of India and notions of India, on Indians in the Caribbean, see Brinsley Samaroo, "The Indian Connection: The Influence of Indian Thought and Ideas on East Indians in the Caribbean", in *Indians in the Caribbean*, ed. I.J. Bahadur Singh (London: Oriental University Press, 1987), 103–21.
53. Bronkhurst, *Among the Hindus and Creoles*, 212. He then calls up poetic corroboration of his triumphalism:

Ours the glory of giving the world
Its science, religion, its poetry and art;

We were the first of the men who unfurled
The banner of freedom on earth's every part,
Brought tidings of peace and of love to each heart.

54. The quote is taken from Bronkhurst, *Origin of Guyanian Indians*, 28. He adds that the Tamils "are the most capable of intellectual attainment, the most susceptible of ambition, the most active, enterprising, and sensitive. Their ancient home was in the Southern extremity of India, extending from Cape Comorin to a little above Madras on the east coast and to Trivandrum on the west. A thousand years before the Christian era this was the most powerful and highly-civilized kingdom of the South. In arts, mechanics, and manufactures, its inhabitants are still pre-eminent. Literature is held in high esteem there." Bronkhurst originated in this region.
55. *Daily Chronicle*, 7 October 1894. This paper carried the following caption in its issue of 13 October 1894: "coolie" WOMAN FOUND DEAD AT GOLDEN GROVE. See also the *Daily Chronicle*, 27 January 1904: BRUTAL MURDER ON THE EAST BANK: A JEALOUS COOLIE'S SHOCKING CRIME.
56. *Report of the West India Royal Commission*, H.W. Norman, chairman (London: Her Majesty's Stationery Office, 1897), Appendix C, Part II, British Guiana, "Statistics Relating to Immigrants" (presented by James Thompson, editor, the *Argosy*). These useful statistics were prepared by W. Alleyne Ireland, sub-editor, the *Argosy*.
57. Ibid.
58. Bronkhurst, *Colony of Guyana*, 250.
59. *Daily Chronicle*, 24 January 1904.
60. As late as 1951–1952, the reaction of black farmers at Danielstown, Essequibo, to Indian success was still rooted in the old perceptions of the nineteenth century. Harold Hickerson, an American anthropologist, observed that "Many Negroes feel that they have been victimised by the East Indians who have accepted lower living standards than [them] . . . . [They] stated bitterly that the wealthiest Indians send their wives into the drainage trenches to catch fish, and do not allow them pillows for their heads or shoes for their feet, and that by such stinting, they were able to save money and thereby set up business establishments and operate their estates" (Hickerson, "Social and Economic Organisation in a Guiana Village" [Ph.D. diss., University of Indiana, 1954], 120).
61. Edgar Mittelholzer, *A Swarthy Boy* (London: Putnam, 1963), 33.
62. Anon., *A Contribution to the History of "coolie" Missions in British Guiana* (Georgetown: printed by W.B. Jamieson, 1877).
63. *Argosy*, 3 June 1893.
64. K.O. Laurence has observed the diverse character of Indian resistance on the sugar plantations: "Starting work late, absenteeism, malingering while under indenture, attacks on estate plant like burning canes and mistreating draught animals, may all be seen as aspects of resistance to the oppressiveness of estate life. Another was the habit of leaving the estate, sometimes in large numbers and complete with agricultural implements, to complain to an immigration officer. For many resistance

took less positive forms: taking to rum was no doubt one of them and in extreme cases so was suicide" (K.O. Laurence, *A Question of Labour: Indentured Immigration to Trinidad and British Guiana, 1875–1917* [Kingston, Jamaica: Ian Randle Publishers, 1994], 491).

65. Ibid., 484–92; Rodney, *Guyanese Working People,* 151–60; Walton Look Lai, *Indentured Labor, Caribbean Sugar: Chinese and Indian Migrants to the British West Indies, 1838–1918* (Baltimore: The Johns Hopkins University Press, 1993), 126–45.

66. In his doctoral thesis of 1977, Tyran Ramnarine unearthed the amazing contribution of Bechu, a seminal Indo-Guyanese leader, or "potential leader". He wrote: "[O]nly one East Indian in the whole nineteenth century appeared as a potential leader. He was unique in that he was not of the local East Indian middle class, and he championed the cause of the downtrodden sugar worker. His name was Bechu, a Bengali, who came to the colony as an indentured immigrant. He became the first East Indian to address a Royal Commission. Not surprisingly he did not obtain his early education in British Guiana. He was educated in India by a missionary. His public criticisms, in the newspapers, of the sugar planters, and his defence of the labourers brought him into conflict with the planting authorities. The manager of Cove and John plantation sued him for libel in a protracted case" (Ramnarine, "The Growth of the East Indian Community in British Guiana, 1880–1920", 233).

See also p. 39, where Ramnarine describes Bechu as the "most famous Indian spokesman and letter writer of the period", the late 1890s, and my *Bechu: "Bound Coolie" Radical in British Guiana, 1894–1901* (Mona, Jamaica: The Press, University of the West Indies, 1999).

67. *Report of the West India Royal Commission,* Appendix C, Vol. II, Part II, British Guiana, Minutes of Proceedings and Evidence.

68. See Ramnarine, "The Growth of the East Indian Community", chapter 3.

69. Quoted in Leader, *Daily Chronicle,* 16 September 1897.

70. Nath, *History of Indians,* Tables 13, 14, 15.

71. Comins, *Emigration from India,* 32.

72. Ibid., 20.

73. *Daily Chronicle,* 29 March 1904.

74. Ibid.

75. One such case was reported from New Amsterdam, Joseph Ruhomon's home town, in September 1900, when Jacob Jaundoo, "an old East Indian [not 'coolie'] resident", died. The *Berbice Gazette,* 12 September 1900, noted: "Deceased, who had attained a ripe age, was a very popular character in this town at one time, and was associated with several financial undertakings. He was a proprietor of a livery stable and a merry-go-round, in Nicolay St., in which street his name has been immortalised as 'Jaundoo Lane'. He came to the colony [from India] when just a boy and by dint of perseverance, rose gradually to a position of prominence. He was interpreter of the New Amsterdam Magistrate's Court, which office he resigned after a time. Deceased leaves a widow and five grown up sons, two of

whom are interpreters in the Immigration Office."
76. Comins, *Emigration from India*, 15.
77. By August 1899, a skilled stratum of Indian workers had emerged at Plantation Port Mourant. An authority of this estate noted: "Of East Indian Creoles other than trained cultivators of the soil, we have no fewer than 5 qualified pan-boilers, and 2 apprentices; 4 journeymen engineers, and 12 apprentices; 2 journeymen carpenters, and 1 apprentice; a sicknurse and a distiller – all of whom earn their living entirely apart from the tilling of the soil. I do not suppose this estate is singular" (*Argosy*, 5 August 1899).
78. Comins, *Emigration from India*, 31.
79. See Frank Birbalsingh and Clem Shiwcharan [Seecharan], *Indo-Westindian* [sic] *Cricket* (London: Hansib, 1988).
80. Comins, *Emigration from India*, 31.
81. The report stated that Asiatic Cricket Club "is a recently organised club of East Indian members only". Their players in this match were: F.E. Jaundoo (captain), Soobrian, J. Lazarus, S. Williams, J. Clement, D.W. Sammy, S. Madray, S. Doobay, L.M. Khan, S. Bacchus, J. Nemdhary. (It is not possible to ascertain whether F.E. Jaundoo was related to Jacob Jaundoo [see note 75], but it is a part of Guyanese lore that all Jaundoos are related.) *Argosy*, 21 December 1895.
82. *Argosy*, 28 December 1895.
83. CO 111/643, Collet to Churchill, no. 161, 27 April 1922, encl.: Memorandum by J.A. Veerasawmy; *Who Is Who in British Guiana, 1945–1948*, 537–38.
84. The newspapers in British Guiana followed the Prince's cricketing conquests with passion, celebrating every manifestation of his excellence. The reverence which he inspired in many Indo-Guyanese would have been enhanced by the following quote which was reproduced in the *Argosy*, 5 August 1899: "The distinctive trait of Ranjitsinhji's cricket is an electric quickness both in the conception and execution of his strokes. Thereby he is able to do such things as a slower eye and wrist dare not attempt. In making the ordinary strokes he differs from the run of batsmen in that he judges the flight of the ball about half as soon again, and can therefore shape for his stroke more readily and with more certainty. At the same time he need not, owing to his marvellous rapidity of movement, allow himself as much margin for errors as others find necessary. And it is this quickness which enables him to take, even upon the fastest wickets, the most unheard-of liberties without fatal results. Who, for instance, but Ranji can hit across a fast ball without either being bowled or making an appalling mis-hit? Yet Ranji finds not the slightest difficulty in doing so. This hook is perhaps his most notable stroke. He has a miraculous knack of turning the ball accurately from the pitch, and flicks it round to the on-side with subtle, yet terrific power . . . There never has been a greater master of cutting and leg-play." (The quote was taken from the famous book, *The Book of Cricket*, edited by C.B. Fry.)
The regal provenance of Ranji ennobled his achievements, lifted their sense of self-worth in this cricket-obsessed colony, and heightened the stature of the game

among Indo-Guyanese.
85. The *Daily Chronicle* of British Guiana, 28 October 1896, reproduced an article, "The Prince of Cricketers", from the *Daily Telegraph* (London). It was occasioned by a banquet at Cambridge University to honour Prince Ranjitsinhji, following his auspicious debut as a Test cricketer for England, in the summer of 1896. The correspondent remarked: "If happily poor Chester Macnaghten, himself an old Cambridge cricketer, had lived long enough to be present in the Guildhall of the great University town tonight, he would have been no true son of Alma Mater if he had not been prouder of the fact that he gave the first lessons to the great pan-Anglican game to Kumar Shri . . . Prince Ranjitsinhji, than of all the other elements of knowledge instilled by him into the mind of his distinguished pupil when a boy student at Kathiawar [in India]. The love of our national pastime thus begotten, has held its sway so strongly against all rivals, that the young Indian prince who celebrated his twenty-fourth birthday in our midst on the 10th of this month [September], is acknowledged, without any disparagement of the great Gloucestershire veteran [W.G. Grace] and others, to be both the finest exponent of the game and the most popular cricketer of the day . . . Although he learnt to play cricket in India when only eleven or twelve years of age, the desire to become a great cricketer only seized him when, in the year 1888, he was taken by his tutor to see the match between Surrey and the Australians at the Oval. In the summer of 1892, by an accident, as he puts it, 'he was pressed into service as a substitute in one of the Trinity matches', for which he got his college cap, to be followed, in the succeeding year, by his 'Blue'. It is a matter of history now how, after having [been] unaccountably left out of the first test match against Australia during the past season [1896], he was unanimously chosen to play in the other two encounters, especially distinguishing himself at Manchester by scoring 62 and 154 not out, when such well-tried men as Grace and Stoddart were comparative failures."

Prince Ranjitsinhji was, to the Indians in British Guiana, not some remote, cricketing prince; he was claimed as a hero, whose mastery could be appreciated in creole society – another expression of Indian excellence to challenge the "coolie" image.
86. See my *India and the Shaping of the Indo-Guyanese Imagination, 1890s–1920s*, 24–25, and Appendix V, 67–68.
87. Ibid., 25–26.
88. *Argosy*, 30 December 1899.
89. *Argosy*, 16 September 1899.
90. Joseph Ruhomon, "Centenary Notes and Comments", *The Indian Opinion*, May 1938, 403. He added: "In spite . . . of all hindrances to their path, Indians in British Guiana as a whole have given a very creditable account of themselves in various directions – have indeed done far more than could reasonably have been expected of them in the circumstances" (p. 401).
91. Peter Ruhomon, "Au Revoir", *Daily Argosy*, 25 October 1942.

PART 2

The Lecture

India; The Progress of Her People at Home and Abroad and How Those in British Guiana May Improve Themselves

INDIA;

THE PROGRESS OF HER PEOPLE AT HOME
AND ABROAD,

*AND HOW THOSE IN BRITISH GUIANA MAY
IMPROVE THEMSELVES;*

BEING

A LECTURE

DELIVERED

IN ST. LEONARD'S SCHOOL ROOM,
GEORGETOWN, DEMERARA,

On the Evening of the Fourth October, 1894,

AND NOW IN A PAMPHLET FORM, WITH SLIGHT
IMPROVEMENTS;

PRESENTED TO THE PUBLIC BY

JOSEPH RUHOMON.

———◆———

GEORGETOWN, DEMERARA:
C. K. JARDINE, PRINTER TO THE GOVERNMENT OF BRITISH GUIANA
1894.

O: 7,000.

INTRODUCTION.

Mr. J. Ruhomon undoubtedly deserves the thanks of the community of people he represents for this his maiden attempt as a Lecturer to appear before the public in the City of Georgetown. He has certainly rendered great service to the East Indian population in this Colony. Though young in years, he is studious and promises to become a man of eminent abilities. The lecture was read to me before it was delivered, and I have since read it with much pleasure as it appeared in the columns of the *Daily Chronicle*. It is on a subject which I have frequently in private and public put before the people amongst whom I am labouring as a Christian Missionary; and my young friend, among many others I have in the Colony, is the first who has had the pluck to come forward in so public a manner to aid and encourage me in my various attempts to benefit the East Indian Community by delivering this well prepared and truly interesting lecture. Young men, West Indian Creoles, Hindoos and Hindo-Guyanians, have in the past been greatly aided by me in an unobtrusive manner, and they today hold respectable positions in the Colony and elsewhere for which I feel grateful, and I am still willing in my humble and unpretending way to render similar assistance if the young Hindo-Guyanians and others would only accept the inducements offered to them. They who would be helped must help themselves. As the great outcome of this lecture I should much desire to see started and established in the Colony a HINDO-GUYANIAN CHRISTIAN AND MUTUAL IMPROVEMENT SOCIETY under the patronage of Christian Ministers. I have indeed great pleasure in giving this lecture my most cordial commendation, as worthy of the patronage of the community in whose behalf and interest it was prepared and delivered.

HENRY V.P. BRONKHURST,
Wesleyan Missionary.

Georgetown, Demerara,
October 22nd, 1894.

INDIA; THE PROGRESS OF HER PEOPLE AT HOME AND ABROAD[1]

I do not know, Mr. President, Ladies and Gentlemen, that any devoted patriot, full of love and enthusiasm for his country and race – the East Indians [2] – has ever before stood up upon a public platform in this Colony to suggest the best way in which his people here may promote themselves intellectually, morally and socially, and in every way to make themselves influential and honourable in the community. This is so far as my knowledge goes. It is true that there have been a few men, possessed with a great desire for the advancement of their people who have done their very best in the past to carry out this laudable object, and with very good results; and even now, I believe, there are one or two good men who are not at all in a disposition to sit down with their arms folded when they can do something to further the interests of East Indians in the Colony. But it is a regrettable fact that the public platform, which I consider the best medium for the diffusion of knowledge – immensely necessary practical knowledge, – is not in the slightest countenanced. The newspaper press is a wonderful and powerful instrument for the bringing about of great reforms, for the stirring up of the masses to lead high and pure and noble lives, and for the dissemination of knowledge which will lead to decidedly beneficial results; but I consider the platform in its own way, even more wonderful and powerful. By means of this splendid vehicle of thought how much of practical good cannot be done! The editor in his sanctum wields that little insignificant instrument that is mightier than the sword – the pen – and achieves conquests that are more glorious than are achieved in the field of battle; but the orator on the platform, by voice and attitude and gesture, enchains and captivates the attention of his audience and enforces his words in a manner that goes right home, burning their way into the hearts and minds of his hearers, producing an impression that is genuine and lasting and effective. Yes, I believe in the potency and influence of the platform.[3] My only regret is that those who are possessed with oratorical powers or what is called "the gift of the gab" do not resort to it at all, when they are conscious of the fact that by so doing they will immensely benefit their own race and earn the gratitude of countless thousands. I feel very proud of the fact of my being here this evening to say a few words to my own people. The interest of my race is dear to my heart as it should indeed be to every loyal son of India here or to those whose progenitors have come from that great country presided over by Her

Gracious Majesty the Queen Empress.[4] I am a warm and enthusiastic lover of my race and the country of my ancestors, and I do not think there is any one who breathes in this room to-night with soul so dead that the interest of his race, and the country of his fathers, have never in however small degree, engaged his attention. Nay, I am sure that you all have this grand spirit of patriotism and love of your own people, and that you would never be found lacking in effort should any occasion arise that would require the advantage of your services, and that you would use your personal influence, social position, and all and every other means at your disposal to work for the enhancement of the highest interests of your race.

One of the most peculiar and striking characteristics of the times, is the spirit of progress. Go wherever you may, from one end of the earth to another, from east to west, from north to south, and evidence is not wanting to show us that the world is deeply impregnated with this spirit. The car of progress is ever marching forward. Mankind is growing wiser, better, and more enlightened under the purifying influence of civilization. There is no more that intellectual and moral torpor or stagnation which existed in the centuries gone by. Humanity is no more to be cribbed, cabined, and confined and their efforts for advancement paralysed, as in the by-gone years, when so many pernicious and dwarfing influences existed to hinder the acquisition of knowledge and individual and national progress. The nations of the world today are infinitely more enlightened in many respects than the nations who lived and died centuries ago, and all on account of the spread of civilizing influences and the grand diffusion of knowledge. In literature, in science, in art, immense progress has been made by the foremost nations in the world, and they have made such splendid records, as have beaten back and eclipsed in splendour all previous ones. Take Europe, for instance; never before in the history of that great continent have there been so many earnest devotees to literature, to science, to art philosophy. The Elizabethan Era was celebrated for the mighty intellectual giants it produced in these domains of human thought and activity – geniuses who have shed such brilliant lights on the world. The immortal and myriad-minded Shakespeare represented the great world of Literature, which today has assumed such wonderfully large proportions, and the collection of works he has written and that has been transmitted to posterity still holds a foremost place in the literature of the world. The arts and sciences were but developing in those distant times – they were but in their infancy, nevertheless they had their advocates, earnest and enthusiastic men, who by their splendid contributions to them, have drawn upon themselves the veneration and admiration of the world. Those were indeed times of a great out-pouring of intellectual power and a sudden awakening up of the world to the bright light of knowledge which has steadily continued to our own times and has increased in brilliancy and in splendour.[5]

But our business is not so much with the past as with the present, the times in which we live. Need I tell you that the world has gone through and is going through an evolutionary process, and that this is the grandest epoch in its history, so far as knowledge is concerned? Need I point out to you the vast and important discoveries made in the realms of science and art, the gigantic strides which literature has made, and the inventions hit upon by the wonderful genius of man? Everything around and about us bears testimony to the fact that this is decidedly an age of progress such as was never before witnessed in the world's history, and the nations are realizing the fact that the true secret of national greatness and power is in the acquisition of knowledge. Look at England today. It enjoys the enviable reputation of being the greatest country in the world. And why? Is it on account of her great military power or her naval supremacy? It is true that in these respects she is deservedly great. But what is it that has given her a leading position among other nations? Why, ladies and gentlemen, it is her great men and great women. It is they who have contributed to England's glory and greatness as a country. It is they who have enriched her literature which today stands second to no other nation's. It is they, who, although they have borrowed from others have widened the boundaries of her science, improved upon her arts, and brought them up to a high state of perfection. But other nations are not to be outstripped by the great English nation. Seeing what England has done and is doing they have been fired into activity. Competition has grown keen and continues to grow keener every day. Other nations are rising up to their high privileges too. They are realizing their high responsibilities, and they are making good use of the times in which they live as is evidenced by the progress they are making in general knowledge, – times when an almost universal peace prevails upon the earth, and which offer such splendid opportunities for the prosecution of those things which conduce to the lifting up of nations and individuals. Take Africa for instance, and you will pardon me if I dwell at some length upon this remarkable country.

Darkest Africa is no more darkest Africa since Livingstone and Moffat and Stanley and Baker and others have gone there and scattered broadcast

Christianizing and civilizing influences that have paved the way for great moral and social reforms. In that once midnight-dark country full of ignorance and superstition and wickedness of every kind, the golden light of knowledge has broken.[6] We find there today a wonderful improvement. The habits and customs of the people have undergone a change. Institutions for the spread of various kinds of useful knowledge have been founded by benevolent and philanthropic men. The natives are being trained in the knowledge and fear of God, and becoming active and useful members of the community, and filling important positions in life. Today, Africa is sending forth missionaries from among her own sons to distant parts of the world to teach others what they themselves have received – a knowledge of the way of salvation. Today, Africa is filling up the great seats of learning in Europe, where her sons are given that broad and liberal education which enables one the more successfully to compete with others in the struggle of life, and where by their aptitude and diligence in their studies they are distinguishing themselves among their European brethren in the carrying away of University honours. Today Africa has her sons in almost every part of the world, filling almost every station in life and, in short, showing themselves to be in intelligence and in mental capacity not a whit inferior to their fair-skinned brothers. Go to the United States of America and there you have a remarkable instance of the progress of the coloured race.[7] Since their emancipation see what the negroes have accomplished. In 1863 (I am quoting from a recent statement) they numbered four millions; in 1890 seven millions four hundred and seventy thousand; in 1863 they could lay claim to no possession, no property of any kind, they had scarcely the barest necessaries of life. "Now in the State of Georgia," says a gentleman, "they have on the tax duplicate fifty thousand pounds. In Louisiana there are thirty-two coloured men whose fortunes vary from six thousand pounds to thirty thousand pounds, and in 1892, a coloured man died leaving an estate valued at three hundred thousand pounds. In the same year the cotton crop of the State of Mississippi was valued at seventy million dollars, about one-half of which was owned by the negro population of the State. At the time of the emancipation it was a crime to teach a negro to read and write. Today over two million negroes can both read and write; and in the common schools of the United States there are about one million three hundred thousand coloured people." Here is another statement, showing the progress of negroes in America. "One died recently leaving $1,000,000. He had been a slave and learnt the tailor's trade. The wealthiest negro in Louisiana is credited with a fortune of $500,000, and the possession of one of the finest libraries of French, Spanish and Italian classics in the State. In Arkansas there are some half-a-dozen negroes, all born in slavery, and now worth $50,000 to $250,000. One of these, a man 60 years of age, is in every respect self-made. He owns the entire street car system in a town of 12,000 people; a sawmill working 60 hands, two good Plantations, besides some valuable rural estates. He is also a Director in the Bank." With regards to education, a recent statement has it, the United States has 47 grammar schools, 25 colleges, 25 schools of theology, 5 medical schools, 5 law schools and thousands of other schools, all for the benefit of the coloured people! They have their newspapers too, all great organs of power, more than two hundred being published in the United States alone and by coloured men. And, ladies and gentlemen, this is the record of a people who only a generation ago were slaves. "Making allowance for their environment," says a writer, "the free negroes have made greater progress in fifty years than any other race in the world." Yes, the whole world cannot deny this fact, which is obvious enough. The negroes are a great people; they have been so from the earliest times, and though there have been many impediments to their progress, they are rising and making their influence felt far and wide. "Will it be believed," says an English writer, "that this race can, as to intellect and genius, exhibit a brighter ancestry than our own – that they are the off-shoots, wild and untrained, it is true, but still the off-shoots, of a stem which was once proudly luxuriant in the fruits of learning and taste; whilst that from which the Goths, their calumniators, have sprung remained hard and knotted and barren? For is Africa without her heraldry of science and of fame?"

As I have already remarked, Africans have been famous from the earliest times. "The only probable account," says the writer I have just quoted, "which can be given to the negro tribes, is, that as Africa was peopled from Egypt by three of the descendants of Ham, they are the off-spring of Cush, Mizraim and Phut. They found Egypt a morass and converted it into the most fertile country in the world; they reared its pyramids, invented its hieroglyphics, gave letters to Greece and Rome, and through them to us (the English nation). The everlasting architecture of Africa still exists – the wonder of the world, though in ruins. Her mighty Kings have yet their record in history. She has poured forth her heroes on the field, given bishops to the Church and martyrs to the fires. Modern times have witnessed in the persons of African negroes, generals, physicians, philosophers, linguists, poets, mathematicians, and merchants, all eminent in attainments, energetic in enterprise and honourable in character."

I need only mention one or two coloured men whose qualifications have raised them up in the world. Take, for instance, the great Frederick Douglass.[8] What was he in early youth, but a poor, uncared for boy with little or no opportunities for improvement, cribbed and cabined and confined as he was. But the unfavourable circumstances under which he was placed were not to be a barrier to his progress. He studied hard, he persevered much, and now today he is reputed to be one of the most learned coloured men in the world and an honour to his race. Sir Samuel Lewis[9] is another of the gifted sons of Africa, who has recently been raised by the Queen to the dignity of a K.C.M.G., an honour which is reserved for Her Majesty's Diplomatic Envoys, Colonial Governors, Premiers and Generals and Admirals; and it is said that it is for the first time that the British order of knighthood has ever been conferred upon an African. I should here refer also to Bishop Crowther[10] and Bishop Walter Hawkins, both of whom rose from slavery to distinguished positions in the church.

My East Indian friends, do not for a moment think that I am depreciating your race and my race when I refer to the coloured people as a great people who are raising by rapid strides to opulence and fame and attracting the attention of other nations. My only object in referring to the advancement of other races is simply to show you that progress is the watchword of the nations, and that the spirit of progress is one of the most prominent characteristics of our times. As I have before remarked, every nation under heaven has made some progress in general knowledge and continues to make progress, and not the least among them is the great East Indian nation about whose progress I have something special to say. You know, my friends, it is by comparisons that we can estimate the real value of things, and it is only by comparing ourselves with other races that we can arrive at the knowledge of what we ourselves are doing in the world, and especially in this Colony of British Guiana.

Two of the greatest nations in the world that have been noted for gross moral and intellectual darkness were Africans and East Indians. Both were renowned many, many centuries ago. Both have had an interrupted career, both have had a break in the course of their progress, with the darkness of ignorance and superstition settling upon them, and both to-day are climbing up the ladder of progress. I have already given you a brief sketch of the rise of Africans, and the positions they are filling in the various departments of life. Now I must talk about my ancestral home – India – the work that is being done there and the distinguished parts her children are playing in different parts of the world.

"The India of today", says a distinguished Colonial writer [H.V.P. Bronkhurst], "is not the India of three thousand or four thousand years ago. People forget that India was once a prosperous and civilized country. All the travellers, Greeks, Romans and Chinese who visited the country, bore testimony to the fact that the Hindus had attained a high state of civilization. Even now there exist in India masterpieces of art which had been a wonder to Europe." And what do these masterpieces of art show us? They show us that civilization was dominant in those early times, that the people must have known the refinements of life perhaps such as are enjoyed by civilized beings to-day, for there have never been works of art, or fine and exquisite workmanship constructed by rude and barbarous minds, but by minds refined and cultured. Some people seem to think that India never knew the arts of civilized life until these latter days of missionary enterprise, and the wide diffusion of European influences. Some people seem to think that a pall of everlasting darkness had settled upon India since she began her history as a nation, and that the light of knowledge had never shone upon her people. But no one who has perused the pages of East Indian history, and actually gone through with a knowledge-seeking mind this great country, and studied the remains of ancient glory and of a departed greatness, can ever for a moment entertain such erroneous thought. But time which always works great changes in the world, laid his hands heavily upon favoured India. Her history took a new course. Her people underwent a transformation. Their life and thought as a nation were changed. Then it was that civilized, enlightened India became uncivilized, barbarous India, and began to engage seriously the attention of Gospel missionaries and social and moral reformers. *Ichabod*[11] was written upon it, for verily its glory had departed.

But, ladies and gentlemen, the time has come, God's own appointed time, for India to reassert herself among the other nations of the world, not only as a land blessed with the civilization she once had, and with intelligent and cultured sons and daughters, but with that light which alone can lift up nations to the high level of true, genuine greatness – the light of the glorious Gospel of our Lord Jesus Christ. Says a writer, "there has been a change for good in the social, moral and religious sense in the conditioning of the people of India for some considerable period, and especially during the past half-century of our beloved Sovereign's reign. European influence, science and learning, inventions and customs, introduced there have so opened the eyes of the people as to make them wiser than they were before in regard to their condition; and the spread of Christianity among them is fast breaking down the caste feeling prevailing among the different tribes of Hindus, and delivering them from baneful superstitions." Says another writer: "British rule and Western education are doing a great deal in India. Many movements, moral and political, now stirring the lives of the Indian people are doing still more. These movements are the direct result of the enfranchisement of thought, the individual security and the freedom of speech and opinion which British rule has secured for India."

It appears as if Providence is allowing every nation to have its chance, to be clothed and etherialized with the glorious light of power-giving knowledge, until at last all the nations of the earth shall be one, all speaking one language (which there is no reason to doubt will be the great English tongue), all living in one grand, common brotherhood, and all acknowledging the fatherhood of God.

Europe today basks in the sunlight of a wide civilization, and all that civilization brings in its train; and so does America, which having begun its course as if it were but yesterday, is already a mighty and powerful country. It is now for Africa and India to take their chance and to rise to the level of the splendid opportunities offered them. Africa, as I have already shown you, is not slow and indifferent to its own interests, but is making rapid strides in her march of progress. India, on the other hand, is not a whit behind her sister Africa.[12] India at the present time looks back with infinite pride and satisfaction at the good work she has already accomplished since her emancipation has been effected – I mean in a moral and social and political sense – and since enfranchisement of thought and speech and action has been accorded her, India is attracting the attention of the whole world. Her marked progress has been a matter for congratulation by some of the greatest writers, and that it is not at all improbable that at no distant future, she will occupy a foremost place among other great countries of the earth. One should only look through our Indian magazines and journals to see what India is really doing, and the present enviable position she occupies. The country is becoming thoroughly Europeanized. Charitable and philanthropic institutions are to be seen from one end of the country to another and are directed by capable and efficient men and women. Societies for the diffusion of knowledge have been established in every centre of importance; colleges and schools of various kinds are simply legion, as are also associations devoted to the intellectual, moral and social welfare of their members, and the great good that these educational institutions are doing can scarcely be estimated. Among Indian societies I need mention just a few of the most important. Take the National Indian Association. Having been founded in England by Miss Carpenter[13] in 1871, it has now many branches in India – in Bengal, Bombay, Madras, Poona, Hyderabad, Mysore, Punjab and Gugerat [sic]. "The object of the Association is to extend a knowledge of India in England, and an interest in the people of that country; to co-operate with all efforts made for advancing education and social reform in India; and to promote friendly intercourse between English people and the people of India." The methods of working of this great society are: (1) diffusing information on Indian subjects by the publication of a monthly magazine and by lectures; (2) grants in encouragement of Education in India, scholarships, gifts of books to libraries, prizes for schools, &c; (3) selecting English and Indian teachers for families and schools, and giving friendly help to teachers visiting England; (4) superintending the education of young Indian students in England; (5) encouraging the employment of medical women in India; (6) affording information and advice to Indians in England, and aiding them in any objects connected with the aims of the Association; (7) arranging soirees and occasional excursions to places of interest. The Branch Associations undertake educational work, and promote social intercourse between English and Indians. Among the many distinguished life members of this Association are H.R.H. the Princess of Wales, the Duke of Connaught and the Earl of Northbrook. The East Indian Institute is another great Association. It is a centre of union, enquiry and research for all interested in India. I believe a society of the same name was founded *here* some time ago, and was directed by some of our prominent East Indians in the city; but unfortunately it had a short career, its mighty colossal pillars gave way, it came down with a crash, and great was the fall thereof.[14] But I must not talk of what is matter only for the historian. An association that is doing very good work in India and is supported by the Indian Princes and aristocracy, is the East India Association.[15] It is an organization of Anglo-Indians and native gentlemen established "for the disinterested and independent advocacy and promotion by all legitimate means of the public interests and welfare of the inhabitants of India generally." Sir Richard Temple,[16] I think, is the President. Too much praise cannot be bestowed upon the Aligarh Institute, which was founded by Sir Syed Ahmed.[17] It looks after the educational reforms of the Mahommedans. The students have started two societies in connection with the college. One undertakes the philanthropic duty of collecting funds for the support of those students who cannot afford to pay for their education. The other, called the "Brotherhood", has the gigantic task of securing a great fund to ensure the future stability of the College. Perhaps no other man has had so many difficulties and discouragement to contend with, in endeavouring to start a college of this kind, as Sir Syed Ahmed. The Aligarh Institute is an honour to him and will remain as a permanent memorial to his true worth and greatness as a benefactor to his race and country. The Society for the Encouragement and Preservation of Indian Art is a very useful Society. It has, indeed, a noble object, and that is, "to foster the indigenous decorative arts of India and, where it is possible, to help to keep them distinctive. It seeks to do this by encouraging artisans in every province of the country to continue practising their hereditary handicrafts, by extending a taste for genuine Indian art work; by refusing to patronise unsuitable and incongruous western designs, and by other means as occasion arises." Young Men's Christian Associations, Christian Endeavour Societies, and other mutual improvement Societies are all doing good work in India, being great moral and intellectual forces, and powerfully influencing the lives of the people there. So much for Societies and Associations in India.

I pass on now to the genius and industry of East Indians as a people. It is a common saying in this Colony that East Indians have nothing good in them; that they are an inherently lazy and vagabond class; that they are only fit to come over to this Colony as immigrants in ship-loads to till the white man's field to get the white man's money and go back to their country and live a comfortable idle life. But I hope I shall be able to dispel this erroneous impression from the minds of many tonight.

East Indians are an inherently great people, and I feel supremely proud of the fact as one who has the pure, genuine East Indian blood flowing in his veins. In their own literature, science, and art, East Indians have held their own. "Those who have read the history of India," writes a distinguished, grand old East Indian Christian Missionary of many years standing, in this Colony (already referred to on page 5 [p. 54]), "ancient as well as modern, will admit that these people, at least their forefathers, have very largely contributed towards extending our knowledge of nature, in mathematics, astronomy, mechanics, and other sciences such as arithmetic, geography, algebra, etc."[18] Says the same writer, "Indians have produced poets, philosophers and mathematicians, such as Vyas, Gautam, Kalidas, Bhawanbhut, Aryabhat, Basker Acharya, and a host of others, whose original lofty genius is now universally admitted by those who have deeply studied them to be by no means inferior to that of Shakespeare, Locke and Newton, making due allowance however for the remote age in which they flourished."[19] Again, this same writer refers us to "all those grand and extraordinary changes wrought by the Asiatics in the times gone by," which, he says "could be viewed in no other light than that of a prelude to the act in which it has pleased Providence to appoint the long-neglected Britons to take a prominent part since the last century, – changes which were no more than original patterns given on which modern Europeans have made but improvements. If the Europeans have invented printing, steam-engines, railroads, and electric telegraphs, their great boasts in these days, perhaps *vox et præteria nihil* – it was the Asiatics who invented and taught their masters the very letters which they now print, the first principles of mathematics, astronomy, chemistry, and mechanics, which contributed so largely to the development of these modern inventions".[20]

Again, this writer refers us to India as "a country which has produced such conquerors and statesmen as Zenghis, Teymoor, Baber, Akbar, Shivajee, Bajeerow, Nana Pharnavis, Mahadjee Sindhia, and a host of others – a country which has produced poets, legislators, statesmen, divines, philosophers, astronomers, and mathematicians, equal or perhaps superior to those of any other civilized country on earth – a country which has produced men, in those rude days of the past, whose minds could conceive the idea and execute the plan of such noble, stupendous and elegant works as the excavations at Ellora, Elephanta, and several other places in India; the various hill-forts of great magnitude, in places high and difficult of access in the Deckhan [sic]; the beautiful temples and pagodas – such as Trimal Naikh's Tank and Palace, the Choultry, (a splendid granite hall 333 feet by 82, on 128 stone pillars); the Tyanana Swamy Pagoda, 300 feet high; the great 14 storey Pagoda of Tanjore, built in the 11th century; the massive granite pagoda, 1,000 feet by 660 feet, at Rameswaram on the Couramandel Coast – scattered throughout the length and breadth of India; and last, the elegant and magnificent arches near Delhi, the Tajmahal at Agra, the great canal of Joan-poor [sic], and numerous other works of civil and military architecture."[21] India has been celebrated for its architecture. There are temples in Conjiveram, Srerangam, Madura and other places which are lasting monuments of the native's fitness for the construction of works of real magnificence.

"Near to Jaganath" says Abdul Fazal,[22] "is the Temple of the Sun, in the erection of which was expended the whole revenue of 12 years. No one can behold this immense building without being struck with amazement." Writing about the Taj, Mr. Fergusson says:—"Perhaps in the whole world there is no scene where nature and art are so successfully combined to produce a perfect work of art as within the precincts of the far-famed Mausoleum. No words can express the chastened beauty of that central chamber seen in the soft gloom of that subdued light that reaches it through the distant and half-closed openings that surround it. Used as a Burrah Durrie or Pleasure Palace, it must always have been the coolest and loveliest of garden retreats; and now that it is sacred to the dead, it is the most graceful and the most impressive of the sepulchres of the world."[23] In art, India has acquired sufficient excellence to excite the admiration and envy of other nations more exalted and more renowned.[24] In the potter's art, great improvements have been made by Indians. The work of Indians in gold and silver, for practical use and artistic effect, is said to be unequalled. In the making of arms they have acquired a very great reputation. The Prince of Wales' collection of Indian arms is celebrated for its variety, extent, gorgeousness and ethnological and artistic value. The choice of fabrics of cotton, silk and wool has been the immemorial glories of India. Cloths of exquisite fineness and delicacy are manufactured in that country. From the earliest times Hindus were celebrated for their knowledge of the arts of handspinning, weaving and printing cotton, and of making the finest muslins; whereas we find that the art was introduced into Europe only so late as the 17th century. "The Indian Fabrics were so fine and yet so temptingly cheap," says Mr. S. Varadacharyar, "that their importation into England alarmed her silk and woollen manufacturers, and as a consequence a law was passed in 1701, forbidding the further importation of Indian goods into England." It is said that owing to the manufacture of cotton goods in England, the trade has suffered considerably in India; but it is hoped that with the rapid development of machinery and manufactures in India, she may yet be able to produce her own cloths even more cheaply than in England, and compete with her in home and foreign markets. In carpets, India is said to be the motherland, and it is only in recent times that they were introduced into Europe. "Indian carpets are noted for their beauty of design, and super-excellence of fabrication and evenness, and fastness of colour. There are several other arts, such as painting, wood-carving, stone-carving, ivory-carving, enamelling, damascening, embroidering and lace works too numerous to be mentioned, but in each and all of which there is abundant evidence to show that the Indians have held their own among other nations of the world. "In a word," – I am again quoting from Mr. Varadacharyar – "the natives of India have exhibited unwearied industry, remarkable patience, admirable ingenuity, sound artistic taste, unrivalled excellence in their art manufactures from the very commonest pottery to the most precious jewellery."[25] In literature, India can boast of her own, and many great works of her great writers have been translated into the English and other languages. India, as has already been shown, has had her poets too, and they have left us many valuable productions, all indicating their authors to have been geniuses of the highest sort.[26] And at the present day, powerful and living poetry is coming into existence – Hali being said to be the leader of this new spirit. Mr. Ramaswami, B.A., Barrister-at-law, has just written a poem consisting of 25,000 stanzas describing the origin and progress of British power, and it is said to be a work of much literary merit.[27] Many people seem to think that there is no real music in the soul of the East Indian: hear what a writer of some experience says:–"Europeans leave India with the idea that the national music of India consists only of noise and incessant drumming, varied perhaps by nasal drawlings equally repulsive as unmusical. That there is a real musical art, with the employment of various scales, abounding in rhythmical beauty and full of passionate expression seems to many almost incredible."

Having, I think, given you a fair idea of the greatness of East Indians as a people, – their genius, their intelligence and their industry, I must now briefly touch on the part, the distinguished part, that India's children are playing in the world today. In their own country, native Indians have proved themselves to be qualified to hold positions that are held by Europeans. As doctors, ministers, legal practitioners, politicians, authors, editors of newspapers, &c., they are certainly not inferior in ability to the Europeans. On the contrary, they have proved themselves to be equal in ability, if not superior, to their fair-faced brothers. They have indeed drunk deep draughts at the fountain of European thought and learning, and there is no question about their being beaten in competition with Europeans.[28] The time is fast coming when the Indians will be able to live independently of British rule, will have the powers of Government thrust into their own hands, and will know how to look after their own affairs and take care of themselves. The time may be far away, but it is as surely approaching as the judgement day. In almost every department of life in India, Indians are to be found engaged, and they are making their influence felt all over the globe. In Europe they are no less clever and pushing, and influential. From Bengal, from Bombay, from the Punjab, from Burmah, from Madras, and other places, Indians of both sexes are to be found in England at the present time all bent upon various pursuits. Yes, both sexes, for the women of India are becoming just as great in the various walks of life as the women of England or of America.[29]

In the early part of this year there were twelve Indian ladies in Great Britain, several of whom were studying medicine,[30] while one was an artist. We cannot at present tell the number who had previously been trained in the Universities of Europe for the professions, and who now are doing good work in different parts of the world. Some time ago I had the very great pleasure of reading a book entitled *Daughters of America*, the writer of which gave a splendid and glowing account of the work of the women of that mighty country.[31] I trust that the time is not far distant when the world shall know the work of our noble East Indian ladies in the publication of a similar volume entitled "Daughters of India." Among well-known Indian gentlemen in Europe, I saw in a recent publication that there is one, a professor in Trinity College, Dublin; one, a teacher in Liverpool; and one a translator, and another a teacher in London; and one, a Missionary in Glasgow; all married to English ladies and settled in Great Britain. Hafiz Abdul Karim, Minister and Indian Secretary to Her Imperial Majesty the Queen, ought to be well known to many here as one who by his excellent character and high intellectual attainments, has the distinguished honour of being the confidential servant and friend of the greatest Sovereign in the world. But I must not omit to mention one grand, distinguished East Indian in England, the "Grand Old Man of India", as he is appropriately and affectionately called by his host of admirers – I mean Mr. Dadabhai Naoroji, M.P.[32] I suppose many of my friends here have heard of Mr. Naoroji, and who has not? The first Indian gentleman who has ever been elected to Parliament. He was formerly a Professor of Mathematics and Natural Philosophy. Having left Bombay when he was a young man to seek his fortune in England, he soon by his splendid abilities and sterling character, made his reputation in that country and raised himself up to the exalted and honourable position he now occupies as the representative of his country in the British House of Commons. In this – the greatest assembly in the world – Mr. Naoroji speaks with an authority on Indian matters which certainly no one else can claim, and the great boons he has been the means of conferring on his country, have in great measure led to his endearing himself to his country. We have a striking instance of the high esteem in which he is held by his own people who are justly proud of such a noble son of India.[33] After a very long absence he returned to his native country in January last, and he was accorded a welcome, it is said, that probably transcended anything that India had ever granted to any man since she came under the rule of Great Britain. "The visit of Mr. Naoroji to India," says a paper, "has been marked by great enthusiasm, and his reception particularly on arrival at Bombay was very striking. The route from the Bunder to his residence was all along decorated with Venetian-masts, flags, mottoes and festoons of flowers, and he drove among thousands of people lining the route at windows and on roofs; while bands played, addresses were presented, and school-children sang songs of welcome."[34] Large crowds welcomed him also at other cities on the route to Lahore, in which latter place, says another paper, "the reception he received has perhaps not been surpassed since the days of Runjitsingh."[35]

Our earnest prayers as East Indians should be that not only may this good man long live to be an honour to his race and country, but that God may raise up other Naorojis who shall be instrumental in furthering the interests of, and pouring down streams of blessings upon, our glorious Fatherland.[36]

In many other parts of the world, East Indians are thickly scattered, and by their urbanity, courtesy, steadiness and intellectual ability, they always succeed in holding their own against others. We, East Indians, should feel supremely proud of the fact that the members of our own race are practically showing the world today by their example that the great East Indian nation is no mean nation. Our people have been great in the past and they will be greater yet in the future. The signs of the times point to the brilliant future of the East Indian race. Let prejudiced-eaten races say what they will and false pessimistic prophets; but we know that there is a golden harvest to be reaped by East Indians. In the many walks of life our people are playing most distinguished parts and prominently bringing themselves before the world, in spite of the difficulties and discouragements and obstacles in the pathway of their progress. East Indians have these two grand qualities in them – patience and perseverance – to a very high degree, qualities which are enabling them to overcome all difficulties and surmount all obstacles.

Not a very long time ago, I must confess, I was utterly insensible to the real progress of my race in India; about whom I should have known a great deal more than of any other race. But I accidentally had a plunge into East Indian Literature, – books, magazines and the like devoted to the interest of my race in the great big world. Men of note – learned and famous men –

were brought prominently under my notice. I saw that India was remarkably progressing and her people getting wiser. I saw that India could boast of great men and great women – great thinkers and great writers – as great as any that Europe or any other country has produced – poets, philosophers, scientists and so on. I saw that she had also among her list of celebrities, orators as eloquent as any produced by Greece or Rome, or England, or America, – orators which I thought could hardly be found among Indians – a people which I considered utterly devoid of the splendid gift of the English "gab", and my soul was thrilled through and through with genuine pleasure and admiration when I learnt that there were many brilliant East Indian lights in the world of English oratory; who were Burkes and Pitts, and Gladstones and Talmages, in the glorious Anglo-Saxon tongue – a striking instance of which was afforded us when, at the Great World's Parliament of religions held in Chicago a few months ago, some of our East Indian orators who stood up on the platform as champions of their own religions, simply electrified the vast audience by their marvellous exhibitions in English oratory.[37]

Today I am not only convinced, as I am sure all of you in this room tonight are, of the greatness of India as a country, and the greatness of her sons and daughters as a people, but I am joyfully and confidently anticipating the time when in intelligence, in culture, in morals and intellectual attainments, the great East Indian Race shall be second to none in the world. Yea, I may add here that we also in British Guiana with all our ancestors in India are closely allied by blood relationship to the British nation, as the following Poem by Ben Elvry entitled "To India," extracted from "Lays of the Federation of Greater Britain" will show:-

Brave brothers, of the sun-kissed face
Heirs of the ancient Arya name;
Like heritage with you we claim,
Our tongue betrays our kindred race.
Far sundered had our wanderings been,
By depths of dusk and ways unknown;
Glad now we join once more to own
One Mother Empress – Kaisar – Queen.
Forgive us that we did not know
Our brotherhood when first we met;
That erst as foemen we were set,
Whose present hearts with kinship glow.

Our scholars keen, your pundits sage,
A victory beyond war have won;
Though prehistoric sire and son
Unveiling our joint lineage.
Though mystic lore you sought to prove,
While noisier strife our pulses stirred,
Our aims lay summed in self-same word
To higher light we both would move.
So when your studious sons are brought
To test with us our good or ill,
And grasp with sympathetic skill,
At once our language and our thought
One task shows clear, all else above,
Our equal band in either land,
As helpmates strong and first to stand,
Enlinked in fellowship of love.
Allied by spirit, knowledge, blood,
With gathering force our fates shall blend,
Firm moving to one noble end
Of unity – of ceaseless good.[38]

The second part of my lecture now takes a practical turn and refers to the most important question: "How may East Indians in British Guiana improve themselves?" Having spoken of the progress of India's children at home and abroad, and having shown you that with regard to intellect, or brain power, or mental ability, the race is not inferior to any other, I come down to our own Colony.

It has always been a matter to me for deep regret and gloomy, at least not happy, reflections, that the East Indian race in British Guiana is absolutely in a passive state so far as progress is concerned. Scarcely any signs at all are to be seen of the intellectual and social advancement of our race. What are East Indians in this Colony doing to improve themselves? I do not like to make a sweeping assertion, but I am deeply conscious of the fact, and I am sure many in this audience will agree with me when I say with a clear and unbiased mind that East Indians are doing practically nothing to improve themselves morally, religiously, intellectually and socially, and in every way to make themselves influential and honourable in the community here. We look around and about us and what do we see? Why, that we are in a neutral and passive, if not a retrogressive state, that we are allowing others in the Colony to climb up the ladder of progress, whilst we ourselves remain dormant, ineffective and indifferent.

In British Guiana there is eminently a cosmopolitan community. We have here almost every nationality under heaven. But the two principal nationalities are the descendants of the great African race and East Indians, by which you will please understand me to mean not only natives of India, but those born in the Colony of East Indian parents, and known as Hindo-Guyanians.[39] The African race or the coloured people, as they are popularly called, are distinguishing themselves as I have already told you, not only in their own country – Africa – but in other parts of the world, and even in this Colony of British Guiana, where a half-century ago the forefathers of the present rising black people were plunged in the horrors of slavery. Here, intellectually, morally, religiously and socially they are wonderfully improving, in spite of numerous difficulties and discouragements and obstacles in their way, and the abominable and much-to-be-deplored racial prejudice which is so firmly rooted in the community. Some fifty-odd years ago the black man was the white man's slave in this Colony. He was not counted as a human being, and was treated as a beast of burden by his tyrannical master. He had not the same advantages and privileges that his white brother had. He had no opportunities for raising and improving himself. But the short period of half-a-century has worked a great change in the patient, plodding, ambitious and resolute black man. Today, he is free and untrammelled from the gyves of moral, intellectual and political serfdom. Nothing can now contort and cripple the giant might of his nature and hinder him in his march of progress. In the pulpit, our coloured brothers can hold their own; at the bar they are astute debaters and sound common-sense practitioners; as "medicos" they seem to be masters of their profession, and in many other departments of work in this Colony they are acquitting themselves in a manner creditable to themselves, and the pushing, aggressive race from which they have sprung. The young coloured people have their interests fairly well looked after. Their parents are wise in seeing that they get the educational training, however little it may be, which is given at our public schools, and that they make good use of their time. Those who can afford it, without the slightest stint or niggardly spirit, send their sons to the Queen's College, or the High Schools, in which institutions they qualify themselves to go in for the professions in Europe, and afterwards return to the Colony where they make themselves quite at home – being comfortable and happy in a large and lucrative practice. Our young coloured people here are to be commended on the many societies they have for their own intellectual, moral and social welfare. They have their Temperance Societies, their Mutual Improvement Societies, their Y.M.C.A.s, their Christian Endeavour Societies, and other associations, all of which are living pioneers for good and fountains of beneficial influences. For all this I think our coloured people in British Guiana are to be heartily congratulated.[40]

But our Hindo-Guyanian people in this Colony – O! how regrettable, – are making but very slow progress. They may have opportunities for improving themselves but, alas, they are indifferent to their own interests. They do not know what it is to cultivate the barren wilderness of their minds and the great good that would accrue therefrom. They do not know what it is to acquire an encyclopaedical knowledge or a large fund of that general knowledge which would give them that power which a barbarous uncivilised savage can never have. I like always to make clear unvarnished statements and to call a spade a spade. My Hindo-Guyanian friends, what have you done in this Colony (which indeed is your birthplace) for which you can justifiably congratulate yourselves? Where are your ministers and lawyers and doctors – sons of the soil? In how many public places do we find East Indians engaged and distinguishing themselves? What Hindo-Guyanian do we find in the Court of Policy to represent his own race in the Colony and to manfully fight for the promotion of their interest and the betterment of the condition of the great majority of our people?[41] What societies have you established for the intellectual and moral, social and religious uplifting of your own people? Alas, we cannot congratulate ourselves in a conscientious manner. We have done nothing in the Colony that has redounded to our credit. And why? My friends, do you want an answer? It is because you have no ambition for the elevation of your race and for the union which will pave the way for their emancipation. You have not the grand, world-stirring enthusiasm amongst yourselves. You have not that closer union amongst yourselves which is so essential to the improvement of your race, that union which acts as a lever for the uplifting of nations and individuals. I think there is a great lack of brotherhood or fraternity amongst ourselves, the members of the East Indian Race, and you know where distrust and uncharitableness and hatred are rife, there is no possibility of making any progress in any direction, for they bring forth after their kind, and the result is most unfavourable and pernicious.

Now, my Hindo-Guyanian friends, what is it that is wanted if we are to be improved individually and as a people in this Colony? Why, a wide brotherhood amongst ourselves, a grand spirit of living, burning enthusiasm, and the splendid quality of unity and co-operation – active co-operation – amongst ourselves that would enable us to work together for the common good of our race and the promotion of its highest interests. Let us keenly realize this fact, my friends, that East Indians in general in British Guiana are in a deplorably unprogressive state and they need a helping hand. Leave them to themselves until doomsday and they will have made absolutely no progress. But give them a push – encourage them by every means in your power – and throw out to them certain inducements and you will find no other people in British Guiana more willing to help themselves, and improve themselves to the best of their abilities than the offsprings of East Indians. What a great pity it is that our people in this Colony are so very little cared for, even by those who are appointed as it were, guardians over them! The poorer classes of our people are simply "no-bodies" in the community. On our sugar estates they are no more thought of than the mules which draw along the cane punts. They are severely handicapped in the struggle for existence.

Here we find one of the greatest drawbacks to the progress of East Indians in the Colony.

But, my friends, because our people in this Colony and their children are so very little cared for by their employers or those who are in authority over them, should that be adduced as a reason for their not improving themselves and of making progress individually, and as a people? No; decidedly not. Our people have suffered greatly in the past – they have been simply tools in the hands of their employers, and their interests have been sadly overlooked or neglected. But it is high time now that they awake to their own interests, and put forth their best efforts towards improving themselves in this Colony. Our people must be bold, strong, fearless, acquitting themselves like men. Never be afraid, my friends, of the derisive criticism of your enemies, or the sneers and scoffs of pessimists, and the many barriers which may stand in your pathway when you are striving honourably and worthily and nobly to better your condition and to improve yourselves. Learn a lesson from the example of others and you will promote your interests. Do not think that on account of the racial prejudice rampant in this Colony you can never improve yourselves. I do not see why you should not if you take an interest in yourselves, and are firmly, resolutely resolved, that come what may, nothing can hinder you from reaching the summit of your ambition. Believe me, my friends, if you have not got goaheadness in you, courage and that quality which we call pluck for the possession of which the great English nation are justly renowned, and our coloured people, too, you can never succeed in whatever you undertake.[42] Those of you who are influential and powerful in the community, do the very best you can for the advancement of your own race in British Guiana.

My intelligent and cultured friends, do you know that you can do a great deal in this direction, and that upon you depends the future prosperity and greatness of our race in the Colony? The great majority of our people are weak and ignorant. Stretch forth to them a helping hand. The East Indian race in British Guiana has not yet begun its history as a race. Its past has been chaos and darkness. Our people *shall* be great and *must* be great in the future if you work together co-operatively and in unity, and if you strive to bring about this end, they shall participate in all our industries and considerably contribute to their development, and they shall, in common with others, engage in all the various functions of life in the Colony.

Upon parents of children there hangs a great responsibility – for, as a writer has well remarked, they are personally responsible to the coming generation for the fight it will have to make and for the strength they transmit to it to make that fight. And they can discharge this great responsibility by seeing that their children are educationally well equipped for the battle of life. They should see that their sons and their daughters[43] – the future men and women of the Colony – get, not only that education which would enable them only just to eke out a common living in the future, but that sound, broad and liberal education, which would make them mighty pillars of the fabric of Society, and fountains of goodness from which every gracious and beneficial influence shall flow, that shall continue to permeate the hearts and minds of thousands long after you have quitted this mortal stage.

In the interest of our young men and young women, I have something very important to say. I consider it a downright shame, highly reflecting upon those who ought to assist the helpless – I mean our East Indian aristocracy – that as yet, our young people have no societies whatever of any kind in the Colony, and it is no wonder that we find so many who are devoid of that polish of mind and character which friendly societies impart and to such a very high degree. The young Hindo-Guyanians scarcely have any means at all for intellectual, moral, and social improvement, and innocent healthy recreation, and one of the most prominent thoughts, which suggested themselves to my mind in preparing this, the second part of my lecture, was that I should impress deeply upon the minds of my influential and philanthropic friends the necessity – the great necessity – there is for the formation of societies in our Colony devoted to the intellectual, moral and social well-being of their members. You know very well, my friends, the immense and paramount value of societies of this kind, how powerful they are for good, and their influence how far-reaching. You know the great good they are the means of effecting in the world today. Now, suppose you started one in this city of Georgetown – it could have branches in other parts of the Colony, and there would be practically no end to the immense good it would do by promoting the highest interest of our race here. It is to be deeply regretted that the society which was started in this town some time ago for the benefit of East Indians became so early a total wreck; and I am sure that if that society had been established upon a proper basis and conducted on proper lines its premature death would not have been recorded in the annals of Colonial East Indian enterprise.

But because the East Indian Institute has come to crash is that any reason why you should not make another attempt? I am sure when you can in any way advance the interest of your own race you will not sit still with your arms folded, but will readily adopt those means which will bring about this noble end, and when I tell you, in all sincerity, that a society of the kind I have mentioned is one of the best and most proper means of bringing it about, I am sure you will not think I am talking trash. Just see of what immense benefit such a Society will be to its members. It will be a borough of information; a great centre of beneficial influence. Its members will have an opportunity of meeting together periodically for mutual exchange of thought and social intercourse, &c, and in this way they will be wonderfully improved socially and their ideas greatly expanded and their general knowledge of men and things increased. This ideal society can have both home and foreign papers, &c. Thus its members will be able to know of all the important transpirings in the outside world and have a tolerably fair idea of the progress of the world. If a library is started in connection with the society – a library of the best books in the world and of a pure elevative moral tone, – members would be all the better for it. Books are one of the greatest blessings in life, and the educated mind which dives into literature, enjoys a pleasure of which the rude uncultured mind knows nothing. This society can also provide innocent, healthy amusement for its members, which will be a counter attraction to the debasing and demoralizing so-called amusements of this dissolute age. And lastly, if a newspaper be published periodically as an organ of the society, it would add, I need not tell you, considerably to its usefulness and redound to the eternal credit of the promoters, for the newspaper press today is one of the greatest forces in the world and a mighty power for good.[44]

In conclusion, I have one word for my Hindo-Guyanian friends here. Are you enthusiastic patriots for your country or lovers of your ancestral home, and do you take a real, genuine interest in your people? Then I am sure you will do all that you possibly can by tongue, by pen, on the platform and through the printing press, by exhortation and by practical, tangible help, to promote and advance their interests in this Colony of British Guiana where our people are so little cared for and their interests so sadly neglected. But let me say this, you can never promote the interests of others until you first strive to promote your own.

Life is business, it is real, it is earnest and does not consist in eating and drinking and fun and frolic and pleasure. You have got to be impressed with this tremendous fact that you are personally responsible for your own lives; see to it then that they are being properly spent and in such a way as would redound to your eternal credit. Do not remain idle whilst the hours are speedily fleeting away but rise up to the level of your grand opportunities. You have the glorious gift of intellect – cultivate it by the numerous means which are at your disposal and you shall enjoy a pleasure that is genuine and lasting and true. Life is short, but what a world of good you can do before you shake off this mortal coil. In association with our young women – and woman, you know, is one of the most important factors in society, and one of the most powerful of the forces at work in this 19th century, not only for the emancipation of her sex but in the common cause of humanity – in association with them, I say, you will obtain far better results in seeking to advance your own interests and the interests of our people than you can by working alone. Work together, then, with heart and hand, my Hindo-Guyanian friends, earnestly and enthusiastically I appeal to you. Cast aside pride of intellect and pride of soul which militates against everything that is noble and good, and march on bravely forward, all possessed with one common object, the noble object of promoting the interests of our race in British Guiana, and by your good work in the great cause you shall not only earn the gratitude of countless thousands, but shall draw down upon yourselves the blessings of generations yet unborn.

NOTES TO PART 2

1. This pamphlet is almost the verbatim text of the lecture which Joseph Ruhomon delivered in St Leonard's Schoolroom on Thursday, 4 October 1894. It was reproduced in the *Daily Chronicle* in three instalments: the first appeared on 7 October 1894, covering the lecture from the start to the end of the first paragraph on page 9 of the pamphlet. However, the last line of the first paragraph on page 7 was not included in the *Daily Chronicle*. It reads "I should here refer also to Bishop Crowther and Bishop Walter Hawkins, both of whom rose from slavery to distinguished positions in the church." The second instalment appeared on 12 October, starting from the second paragraph on page 9 and ending at the second to last line on page 20 of the pamphlet. It did not include the last line, commencing "Yea, I may add here . . ." nor the poem, "To India", which ends on page 21. The third instalment appeared on 13 October; it covered the rest of the pamphlet, with a few differences. In the original, Ruhomon refers to creole Indians or Indians born in British Guiana as "East Indians". In the pamphlet, on pages 22–24, he refers to them as "Hindo-Guyanians", a change obviously prompted by Revd H.V.P. Bronkhurst (see the introduction to the pamphlet and note 37 of my introduction). There is one notable omission from the pamphlet. Most of the second paragraph on page 25, beginning "Here we find . . ." was deleted. The *Daily Chronicle* had printed it in full as follows: "The relation existing between master and servant is not as it should be. A great gulf is between them, and the line of distinction between the two is well marked. This is one of the characteristics of our times. That the master shall be above and the servant below – that the servant shall be a slave to his white master, that he shall keep at a respectful distance, and that, if he is to retain his menial position, he should never devote his master's time to self-improvement, or think about pushing himself up in society. There is absolutely no sympathy between the white master and his East Indian servant in many of our places of business, and consequently we find a great barrier placed before him in seeking to improve himself in life, and in every way to ameliorate his condition."
2. The term, "East Indians", which Ruhomon uses to refer to Indians in British Guiana, as well as to Indians in India and elsewhere, was devised in the Caribbean to distinguish Indians from India, and their descendants, from the indigenous Indians, the Amerindians, as well as from Africans or Creoles, who were usually designated "West Indians". Ruhomon never uses "coolie", even when he is speaking of menial workers on the sugar estates.
3. Ruhomon would have been impressed by the oratorical gifts of several of the African and coloured Christian ministers in British Guiana. Reports of Vivekananda's magisterial expositions in English at the Parliament of Religions in Chicago in September 1893, would have deepened his belief in "the potency and influence of the platform".
4. There would have been no contradiction between Ruhomon's pride in India and her ancient heritage and his virtual deification of Queen Victoria, Empress of

India. See my *India and the Shaping of the Indo-Guyanese Imagination, 1890s-1920s* (Leeds: Peepal Tree Books/University of Warwick, 1993), 29–31.

5. This fascination with intellectual endeavour stayed with Joseph Ruhomon throughout his life. Nearly forty-four years after his 1894 lecture, in an address to the [Wesleyan] East Indian Young Men's Society, he was still extolling the superiority of the "higher planes": "[L]ife even at its best was hollow, incomplete, fragmentary, if unrelated to those higher planes . . . one will have failed to achieve one's true destiny if in one's whole life the things pertaining to those higher planes had not engaged one's attention or somehow have been excluded from it" (*Daily Chronicle*, 23 February 1939).

6. Although these remarks are rather strident, he does not belabour the point. Ruhomon is quick to advance and celebrate manifestations of progress, in Africa and India.

7. I am grateful to Peter Fraser for notes 7 and 8. He writes: "During the brief period of Reconstruction, after the American Civil War (1866–1877), African Americans enjoyed political rights. With the return to power of racially motivated White governments in the ex-slave states from 1872 onwards, a process completed in 1877, African Americans were disenfranchised and found themselves subject to discriminatory legislation. Supporters of African Americans, like Ruhomon and the authors he read, could by the 1890s point only to a few politically prominent African Americans, and thus tended to emphasize material progress" (personal correspondence).

8. Peter Fraser notes: "Frederick Douglass (1817–1895) was the most famous African American of the nineteenth century. An abolitionist who visited Britain before the American Civil War (1861–1865), he later held various public offices in the US government, including Minister to Haiti. He wrote three versions of his autobiography of which the first, *Narrative of the Life of Frederick Douglass* (1845), and the last, *Life and Times of Frederick Douglass* (1881), are most worth reading" (personal correspondence).

9. See Fred W. Hooke, *Life Story of a Negro Knight* (Freetown, Sierra Leone: The Author (?), 1915); John D. Hargreaves, *A Life of Sir Samuel Lewis* (London: Oxford University Press, 1958).

10. The Afro-Guyanese barrister (and later legislator) A.B. Brown had given a lecture on Bishop Crowther to the Plaisance Mutual Improvement Society on 14 March 1892. He said that he had seen and spoken to this extraordinary man in London; and he referred to his founding of several mission stations in the Niger Valley (*Argosy*, 19 March 1892). The same newspaper, a few weeks later, carried another item on Bishop Crowther, "that renowned son of Africa, who was captured when a boy, in a slave ship". It then quoted a South African source, who wrote thus: "We remember listening to this remarkable negro bishop when he held with intense interest an audience of five thousand people. It was a time when 'Darwin Theory' was agitating the public mind. When the deafening applause which greeted him had ceased, he turned to the chairman of the meeting and said, 'My lord, I stand before this vast audience of Christian people as a connecting link between the human race and the chimpanzee!' " (*Argosy*, 30 April 1892).

Notes to Part 2

11. A biblical reference (1 Sam. 4:21) that recurs in the writings of H.V.P. Bronkhurst. The name *Ichabod* means *ignominy*, and its use by Bronkhurst would suggest that glory had passed away.
12. Here, again, Ruhomon is sensitive to the racial diversity of Guyanese society and treats both Africa and India with sympathy.
13. The National Indian Association was, in fact, founded in Bristol, in September 1870, by Mary Carpenter (1807–1877). She was an educationist, penologist and philanthropist; she visited India four times, between 1866 and 1876, speaking and writing on the education of women and on penal reform. She had met Ram Mohan Roy, the great Bengali scholar and reformer, in Bristol, in the early 1830s. The formation of the Association coincided with a second visit to Bristol of another great Bengali thinker, Keshab Chunder Sen (*Dictionary of National Biography* [From the Earliest Times to 1900], vol. 3).
14. Seecharan, *Shaping of the Indo-Guyanese Imagination*, 24–25, 67–68.
15. Dadabhai Naoroji, the first Indian member of Parliament in Britain, was the honorary secretary of a similarly named society, in London. During the 1860s and 1870s, he read many scholarly papers to its members. Some were published in the volume edited by Parekh (see note 32).
16. Sir Richard Temple (1826–1902) was a distinguished administrator in India: lieutenant-governor of Bengal 1874–1877 and governor of the Bombay Presidency, 1877–1880. He was the author of *India in 1880* (London: John Murray, 1880), and *Men and Events of My Time in India* (London: John Murray, 1882).
17. L.S.S. O'Malley has written on the contribution of Sir Syed Ahmed [Sir Saiyid Ahmad Khan] to the synthesizing of Western education and Islam, at Aligahr: "The idea of purely secular education was opposed to the tradition of Islam, and it was feared that its rationalising tendencies would undermine the foundations of faith. But experience had shown that English education was a valuable qualification for admission to, and promotion in, government service, as well as for success in other walks of life, and that by abstention from it, the Muslims had fallen into a position of inferiority to the Hindus. There was a growing realization among an influential section that in their own interests they must fall in line with their Hindu competitors and march with the times. This change of front was due very largely to the enlightened guidance of Sir Saiyid Ahmad Khan, a man of outstanding personality, who was convinced that the adoption of western learning was essential for the welfare of his co-religionists. Islamic culture, however, was to be preserved and harmonized with western learning; education was not to be divorced from religion, and moral training was to go hand in hand with scholastic instruction. The immediate outcome of his efforts was the foundation in 1877 of the Anglo-Oriental College at Aligahr" (L.S.S. O'Malley, ed., *Modern India and the West: A Study of the Interaction of their Civilisations* [London: Oxford University Press, 1941], 93).
18. The "distinguished, grand old East Indian Christian Missionary of many years standing" is Revd H.V.P. Bronkhurst, and the quote is in his *Colony of British*

Guyana, 238–39.
19. This quote is taken from an article, presumably written by Bronkhurst, which appeared in the *Bombay Times*, 14 February 1857. It was reproduced in his *Colony of British Guyana*; the quote is on page 11.
20. Ibid., 12. In the 1894 edition of Ruhomon's pamphlet, the inverted commas are missing from the entire quote.
21. Ibid., 14. The inverted commas at the end of the quote are missing in the original.
22. Ruhomon is probably referring here to Abul Fazl, the brilliant chronicler of the reign of Akbar, the greatest Mughal Emperor (1556–1605). Sachchidananda Bhattacharya notes that Abul Fazl was "a profoundly learned man with untiring industry and commanding intellect. He was a faithful officer of Akbar and was for many years his confidential secretary and advisor. He was not only a courtier and man of affairs but was also a great scholar and learned author. His *Ain-i-Akbari* is a statistical account of Akbar's empire, and his *Akabarama* is an authoritative account of the history of India in Akbar's time" (*Dictionary of Indian History* [Calcutta: Calcutta University Press, 1967]). (See entry for Abdul Fazl.)
23. This quote is taken from James Fergusson, *History of Indian and Eastern Architecture* (London: John Murray, 1899 [1876]), 598. Fergusson, the author of several magisterial works on the history of architecture, was enthralled by the diverse, opulent strands woven into Indian art: "In no other country of the same extent are there so many distinct nationalities, each retaining its old faith and its old feelings, and impressing these on its art. There is consequently no country where the outlines of ethnology as applied to art can be so easily perceived, or their application to the elucidation of the various problems so pre-eminently important . . . They display an exuberance of fancy, a lavishness of labour, and an elaboration of detail to be found nowhere else" (Fergusson, *Indian and Eastern Architecture*, 6).
24. Writing in the early 1960s, the late, eminent Indian historian, K.M. Panikkar, underlined India's stupendous artistic legacy: "Today the art of India is recognised as 'a unique chapter in the history of human endeavour'. Its continued vitality, its astonishing range – especially in the fields of architecture and sculpture – the boldness and vigour of its conceptions, no less than the lasting sense of beauty and power it conveys, has placed the Indian artistic heritage among the major cultural legacies of the world. The architecture that created the temples of Ellora, the rock-cut pagodas of Mahabalipuram and the Bhubaneswar temple of Orissa, the sculpture that conceived and executed the Mathura image of the Buddha and the Trimurti of Elephanta and the Nataraja of Tanjore, the bas relief of the descent of the Ganga at Mahabalipuram, and the painting which had its efflorescence in the haunting world of beauty in the caves of the Ajanta have nothing to fear by comparison with the cumulative achievements of Europe during its entire history. When to this is added the achievements of the so-called Indo-Saracenic schools, of which the supreme examples are the Taj Mahal of Agra and the Ibrahim Rauja in Bijapur, we have a variety and magnificence which may well be claimed to be

without parallel" (K.M. Panikkar, *Essential Features of Indian Culture* [Bombay: Bharatiya Vidya Bhavan, 1964], 20).

25. These quotes are probably taken from S. Varadacharyar, *Indian Art and Industries* (Madras: Srinivasa and Co., 1894). It has not been possible to locate this book. The British Library's copy was destroyed during World War II.

26. Commenting on his renditions in English of extracts from a few of the poems of Kalidasa, "the greatest Sanskrit poet", Professor A.L. Basham observes: "Owing to the structure of Sanskrit, literal translation of classical Indian poetry into English is quite impossible, and we cannot convey the aesthetic effect of a Sanskrit verse. The brief extracts here translated in rhythmic prose give but a faint impression of the rich and closely knit texture of the originals or the wonderful sonority of the language, which, when well handled, with all the arts of prosody and ornamentation, surely has a splendour unsurpassed by any other language in the world. Classical Indian poetry, like Indian music and art, developed along lines of its own and its canons are not those of the West, but it has its own special merits and beauties" (A.L. Basham, *The Wonder that was India* [London: Sidgwick and Jackson, 1967 {1954}], 418).

27. I have been unable to locate this reference.

28. This, however, did not lead to a slavish adherence to European thought; it fed and stimulated imaginative perspectives on their own heritage, as Sir Richard Temple observed in 1882:
"They no longer accept a doctrine, secular or religious, merely because it is a result of European Civilization. They search for new standards of their own outside Europe and its ways. Despite their western preoccupations it is towards their own traditions that their loving gaze is turned. Their study of Shakespeare, Milton, Bacon and Locke does not in the least diminish their reverent allegiance to the Asiatic heroes, poets, saints and law-givers of old" (Quoted in O'Malley, *Modern India and the West*, 92).

29. One of the distinguished women of India who would have given Joseph Ruhomon much pride and hope for the progress of women, was Pandita Ramabai Sarasvati (1858–1922). A Sanskrit scholar and indefatigable social reformer and feminist, she wrote a searing critique of Indian patriarchy and some of its enduring, barbaric attitudes to women. Some women in contemporary India may still see it as a tract of their times. See *The High-Caste Hindu Woman* (Philadelphia: Press of the Jas. B. Rodgers Printing Co., 1887).

30. Ibid. Pandita Ramabai's book carried a memorial note to Anandibai Joshee, MD (1865–1887), who had graduated in medicine from the Women's Medical College of Pennsylvania, in 1886. She was described as "the first Hindu woman to receive the Degree of Doctor of Medicine in any country".

31. See Phebe A. Hanaford, *Daughters of America; or Women of the Century* (Boston: B.B. Russell, 1883). The author's wide sympathies for the contribution of all women would have appealed to Ruhomon: "[T]he nation is indebted for its growth and prosperity as a people, and for its proud position among the nations

of the earth, to its women as well as its men. The women who have wrought quietly in their homes are not forgotten or ignored . . . Each true life whether public or private, which any woman of the century has lived, goes to make up the character and glory of the land and the age" (p. 6).

32. Dadabhai Naoroji (1825–1917), a Gladstonian Liberal, was a Parsee from Bombay. He had participated in the first Indian National Congress (Bombay), in December 1885; he was elected President at its second meeting in Calcutta in December 1886. He was the first Indian to achieve a professorship in India. In the 1850s, he taught Mathematics and Natural Philosophy at Elphinstone College, Bombay. He was, later, professor of Gujerati at London University. Many of his writings and lectures on the Indian condition remain vital to Indian historiography. On 6 July 1892, Naoroji became the member of Parliament for Finsbury; he won by three votes. See Chunilal Lallabhai Parekh, ed. *Essays, Speeches, Addresses and Writings (on Indian Politics) of the Honourable Dadabhai Naoroji* (Bombay: Caxton Printing Works, 1887); R.P. Masani, *Dadabhai Naoroji: The Grand Old Man of India* (London: George Allen and Unwin, 1939).

33. Gandhi, in October 1938, recorded his debt to the Grand Old Man. He had left Bombay for England on 4 September 1888, with a letter of introduction to Naoroji (in London), from a man who did not know the latter. Gandhi recalls: "When I reached London, I soon found that Indian students had free access to the G.O.M. at all hours of the day. Indeed, he was in the place of father to every one of them, no matter to which province or religion they belonged. He was there to advise and guide them in their difficulties. I have always been a hero-worshipper. And so Dadabhai became real Dada to me. The relationship took the deepest root in South Africa, for he was my constant adviser and inspiration. Hardly a week passed without a letter from me to him describing the conditions of Indians in South Africa. And I well remember that whenever there was a reply to be expected, it came without fail in his own handwriting, in his inimitably simple style" (Masani, Foreword, *Dadabhai Naoroji*).

34. R.P. Masani, who was a young student in Bombay when Naoroji returned to the city in December 1893, recalls the historic occasion with amazing fidelity to this account; the triumphalism is unrestrained, but civilized: "There was not a road leading to the Bunder, which was not thronged by hundreds and hundreds of citizens; and everywhere along the route were seen groups of women and children waiting to have a glimpse of the simple man of whose heroic exploits they had heard such fascinating stories. Here, there, everywhere were schoolgirls and schoolboys, with garlands in their hands, ready to greet the man revered as the Rishi [Saint] of India . . . From windows, from balconies, even from house-tops, thousands of dusky faces peered down on the moving throng below, and until the conquering hero reached his home, the sky was rent every minute with cheers and hurrahs. Almost every family and every institution brought their quota of flowers and poured them into the carriage in which he kept standing all along the route, bowing to the people" (ibid., 342–43).

35. This quote by W.W. Hunter (1840–1900), a perceptive chronicler of late nineteenth-century Indian life, and a compiler of the famous *Imperial Gazetteer of India*, appeared in the *Times*, and was also reproduced ibid., 346.
36. Joseph Ruhomon's claiming of Dadabhai Naoroji for all Indians in British Guiana, mirrored the latter's own unwavering pan-Indian instincts. As Naoroji proclaimed in Lahore during his tour of 1893–1894: "I am a Hindu, a Musulman, a Parsi, but above all an Indian. My greatest happiness has been this, that all Hindus, Musulmans, and Parsis have expressed their joy at my return . . . India has a great future before it. I bless India. I bless you" (quoted ibid., 346).
37. Ruhomon is referring, here, primarily to the great Hindu thinker and reformer, Swami Vivekananda (1863–1902), whose oratorical expositions enthralled the Parliament of Religions in Chicago in September 1893. Jawaharlal Nehru has written on Vivekananda's contribution to the regeneration of India: "Rooted in the past and full of pride in India's prestige, Vivekananda was yet modern in his approach to life's problems and was a kind of bridge between the past of India and her present. He was a powerful orator in Bengali and English and a graceful writer of Bengali prose and poetry. He was a fine figure of a man, imposing, full of poise and dignity, sure of himself and his mission, and at the same time full of dynamic and fiery energy and a passion to push India forward. He came as a tonic to the depressed and demoralized Hindu mind and gave it self-reliance and some roots in the past" (Jawaharlal Nehru, *The Discovery of India* [London: Meridian Books, 1956 {1946}], 338–39).
38. A prolonged search for this poem has proved fruitless. Its pronounced Aryan sentiments are congruent with the thoughts of several thinkers in the late nineteenth century: Professor Max Müller, W.W. Hunter, the administrator and distinguished writer on India, and Revd H.V.P. Bronkhurst. The young Joseph Ruhomon would have been exposed to this spate of Aryanism. Tapan Raychaudhuri explains why educated Indians found Max Müller's ideas irresistible: "His linguistic studies stressed the common origin of Indo-European languages and the Aryan races. These theories, translated into popular idiom, were taken to mean that the master race and the subject population were descended from the same Aryan ancestors" (*Europe Reconsidered: Perceptions of the West in Nineteenth Century Bengal* [Delhi: Oxford University Press, 1988], 33). In 1882, W.W. Hunter had expounded: "The forefathers of the Greek and the Roman, of the Englishman and the Hindu, dwelt together in Asia, spoke the same tongue, worshipped the same gods. The languages of Europe and India, although at first sight they seem wide apart, are merely different growths from the original Aryan speech" (*A Brief History of the Indian People* [London: Trubner and Co., 1882], 44). On 19 November 1885, in a paper read before members of the Young Men's Christian Association, Georgetown, British Guiana, H.V.P. Bronkhurst advanced his own version of the Aryan antecedents of Indo-Guyanese: "Heathenism and Superstition have together blinded the eyes of the modern Hindus as to their origin and relationship to the Europeans, but as the preaching of the glorious Gospel sheds light and lustre around them, and enlight-

ens their dark and degraded minds, they will wake up to the fact that they – the Europeans and Hindus – are related to each other, by the closest ties. The descendants of the ancient Aryan-Hindus will claim relationship with the Germans or Germanic races in Europe, and the descendants of the ancient Tar-aryans of Scythio-Shemitic Draudyans [sic], or the Tamil population of Southern India, will claim relationship with the English or the Saxons of Great Britain" (*The Ancestry or Origin of our East Indian Immigrants* [Georgetown, Demerara: The Argosy Press, 1886], 68).

39. This term was coined by Bronkhurst for "children born in the Colony, but whose parents came from India". He adds: "They do not like the term 'Coolie', or 'Sammie' [another pejorative term], applied to them, as they do not claim India for their native or birth place" (*Among the Hindus and Creoles of British Guyana* [London: T. Woolmer, 1888], 17).

40. At a time when it was axiomatic to denigrate Afro-Guyanese for their supposed laziness, spendthrift propensities and general lack of ambition, Joseph Ruhomon extolled many virtues in the lives of his African compatriots.

41. See note 9 of the introductory essay for a sketch of J.A. Luckhoo, the first Indo-Guyanese legislator, elected in October 1916. In the 1890s, there was a paucity of Black legislators, too; the first to be elected to the Court of Policy, in 1896, A.B. Brown, remained a legislator until 1921. When he died in January 1939, Ruhomon, as usual, was magnanimous: "[F]rom my personal knowledge of him, [Mr. Brown] was endowed with those qualities of head and heart that have often in the history of his race accounted for the rise into prominence of so many of its members in America and in the West Indies and British Guiana" (*Daily Chronicle*, 14 January 1939).

42. Ruhomon's celebration of fearlessness, strength and continuity of purpose, mirrors a central theme of Vivekananda, in the 1890s: "If there is a sin in the world it is weakness; avoid all weakness, weakness is sin, weakness is death . . . anything that makes you weak physically, intellectually and spiritually, reject as poison, there is no life in it, it cannot be true. Truth is strengthening" (quoted in Nehru, *Discovery of India*, 340–41).

43. Ruhomon's vision for the Indian people in British Guiana was animated by a passion for sexual equality and intellectual vigour.

44. It is significant that Ruhomon advocated what seemed like secular organizations to foster the "intellectual, moral, and social" advancement of Indians in British Guiana. Bronkhurst, on the other hand, preferred a "HINDO-GUYANIAN CHRISTIAN AND MUTUAL IMPROVEMENT SOCIETY under the patronage of Christian Ministers". See his introduction to the pamphlet.

APPENDIX I

Response of J.R. Wharton [Honorary Secretary of the defunct British Guiana East Indian Institute] to Joseph Ruhomon's lecture, 13 October 1894

The Editor, *The Daily Chronicle*, [Georgetown]

Sir, I desire with your kind permission to make one or two observations with respect to the lecture entitled "India, the progress of her people at home and abroad and how those in British Guiana may improve themselves", the last instalment of which appeared on the 13th inst., in your popular paper.

At the outset I wish to undeceive the consciences of those whose minds suspicion haunts, of any intention on my part to say anything that may not be quite in accord with their taste in this matter, and I assure them and those of the public who may have read the lecture that it is only in a spirit of friendliness that I write.

I am gratefully pleased to see that you have, in the impartial exercise of your discretion, deemed it proper to afford the public a perusal of the lecture *in extenso*, which I hope will not be unproductive of some good, if not in the immediate future – sooner or later in the days to come. Mr. Ruhomon, the young, and I may add, plucky lecturer, has earned the thanks of the East Indians in British Guiana, and deservedly so, and he is to be highly complimented for the intelligent and instructive discourse of which he so creditably delivered himself. One cannot help feeling on perusing it that there is a conspicuously remarkable current of patriotism which is intensified by the dignified and independent language which the lecturer has employed throughout the lecture; and it does one's heart good to be treated in this candid manner. I entirely agree, as indeed all others cannot help doing, with what has been said on the subject and the suggestions that have been made; but alas! if we, or I should rather say, the very few of us who are willing and ready to co-operate in adopting some measure for the betterment of our race in this Colony are to receive that disappointing encouragement which we painfully did with an Institute we started a couple of years ago, things had better be left where they are. The Revd H.V.P. Bronkhurst of this city is just the man for us, and I speak from personal knowledge that he is ready and has often offered inducements to our young men to teach and instruct them, and improve them intellectually and otherwise and has actually done so in the past. Let those who wish to resuscitate the British Guiana East Indian Institute ask Mr. Bronkhurst to become its President and sway the body of the Institute. He is eminently fitted to teach us. But it is all to no purpose writing and lecturing and preaching, for it is a deplorable fact that, although these are probably the best means to reach the heart and understanding of men, still our people require something more tangible to move them into activity to realise their true position as men whom that noble rule, the offspring of the British spirit of our age, never intended to deprive of its civilizing and elevating privileges. The present depressed condition of our commercial world has produced some problems difficult of solution, and if a wise head from amongst our own people can suggest or perhaps solve our own problem of moral and intellectual improvement, I shall be glad to hear of it . . .

I am . . .
J.R. Wharton.

Daily Chronicle, 16 October 1894.

APPENDIX II

The Response of the *Argosy* to the Publication of *India; the Progress of Her People at Home and Abroad* (December 1894)

Mr. Joseph Ruhomon has sent us in pamphlet form the lecture on "India and the progress of her people", which he delivered in St. Leonard's schoolroom on 4 October. The author's aims and desires towards the moral and intellectual elevation of his countrymen, are very creditable to him, and if the lecture had been devoted exclusively to practical suggestions for their guidance in the indicated direction, it would have been more valuable. In an absolutely free country like the British Empire, a Hindoo or a Negro has equal opportunity with the Anglo-Saxon to rise to eminence, granted he has the same capacity for taking pains; but it is in this sternly-necessary qualification that the hundreds of millions of the tropical and sub-tropical races are defective. Here and there in the present day, just as it was in the past centuries, springs up a commanding genius whose exceptional career only throws into deeper shade the utterly blank and purposeless lives of the teeming millions; but it is open to all of us to hope and believe, as Mr. Ruhomon says he does, that in course of time the genius, intelligence and industry of the East Indians as a people, will gain for their country a foremost place amongst the nations of the world. We notice that the lecturer is constantly measuring the East Indian with the Anglo-Saxon, and shewing [*sic*] conclusively, to his satisfaction, that the former is at least the equal of the latter. As doctors, ministers, lawyers, politicians, authors, and editors, native Indians "have proved themselves to be equal in ability if not superior to their fair-faced brothers". Granted this to be true, it is the fair-faced brother who has most reason to rejoice in it. It was he who liberated, as far as he could, both the Negro and the Hindu, and it is he who up till now is pursuing his noble efforts to enfranchise the slaves in Africa, and those little-better-than-slaves, the many millions of the lower East Indians, and this work he is carrying on with precious little encouragement or assistance from the close racial connections of either of these miserable peoples. Instead of overflowing with gratitude to the nation which has served them so well, the liberated, elevated and enlightened sons of Africa and India seem to be possessed with a feeling of truly ludicrous jealousy of the national superiority which has endowed them with such priceless benefaction. Mr. Ruhomon and other ambitious and deserving "brothers of the sun-kissed face" should regard the British as their dearest friends, and look to the source of their racial elevation as the surest quarter in which to find what is best and safest for guidance and emulation. There is as little excuse for jealousy on the one side as there is reason for it on the other. And if – to withdraw our observations into local limits – the day should come when those members of our population, now spoken of generically as Coolies, will be mentally and intellectually qualified to take their seats in the Legislature, we feel sure there will not be a true-hearted British subject in the land who will grudge the sublimated Sammy the proudest distinction it will be in his fellow citizens' power to bestow.

Leader, *Argosy*, 29 December 1894.

APPENDIX III

Obituary: Revd H.V.P. Bronkhurst (1826–1895)

On Wednesday, July 17th, one of our most faithful and earnest workers passed away, the Rev. Henry V.P. Bronkhurst. Though he had been ailing for a number of years, the end was rather sudden and unexpected. He was still up and about on the Friday before his death, but the following Sunday it was evident that there was but little hope of his recovery. He was in great pain and agony for two days before the end came, and unconscious at the time of his death. The news of his death spread quickly and was received with deep sorrow by all who knew him. Mr. Bronkhurst was a very familiar figure in Georgetown, and known by almost everyone. For the last thirty-five years he has been engaged in work among the East Indians whom he loved greatly, and who found in him one who was always ready to stand by them and help in word and deed. One of the most touching scenes in the death-chamber was the service conducted by one of his Hindoo converts in the presence of a large number of East Indians. The sorrow that was written in their faces bore testimony to the great esteem in which their Shepherd was held by them, and to the love they felt for him. It will be well-nigh impossible to find a successor to Mr. Bronkhurst; for, to work among the East Indians, more is wanted than a mere knowledge of the language. Such work needs a man who is able to appreciate and sympathise with the needs and difficulties of a people who are unjustly looked down upon and treated as if they were strangers to the feelings and affections that are common to other mortals.

Mr. Bronkhurst was born on the 21st March, 1826, in the Tanjore District [Madras], where his grandfather, a Dutchman, was judge. When only a lad of fourteen, he understood several different Indian languages, and made himself acquainted with the leading religious teachings of India, especially was he a student of the *Rig-Veda*. At the age of sixteen he left southern India for Australia. After a short stay there he went to the Holy Land where he spent three years, and many of our readers, doubtless, have had ample opportunity of listening to Mr. Bronkhurst's lectures on his travels there. He was a keen observer of men and customs, with an eye for everything that could prove in the least interesting, and was always ready to give to others the benefit of his extensive knowledge and learning in an unamusing [sic] [unassuming] and unostentatious way. From Palestine he went to England, and for some time was engaged as teacher for [sic] Eastern languages, especially Syriac, Sanskrit, and Hebrew, and was also for a time employed at Holloway's Establishment as translator. On the death of the Rev. John E.A. Williams, who was the first Wesleyan Missionary to the East Indians in this Colony, Mr. Bronkhurst was approached by the Missionary Committee to take over the work. He landed in Demerara late in December 1860, and has since then been a most indefatigable worker. In 1867 he was compelled to go to England where he remained a few months for the benefit of his health. His heart was in his work; and even in his declining years, though in feeble health, he would hardly ever fail to discharge his duties as a minister. In addition to his ordinary work, he found time for writing. His many and various contributions, especially those relating to Eastern subjects, have been widely read and appreciated. Mr. Bronkhurst was a man with deep and Christ-like sympathies. Broad in his views and liberal in his concessions, he never allowed any difference of opinion, creed or nationality to stand in the way of rendering assistance whenever it was needed. It was enough for him to hear that anyone was in trouble and he was ready to help. He was also a fearless Christian, and one [sic] would never sacrifice his principles for the sake of public opinion; in short, as far as his whole character was concerned, he was a man worthy of imitation. His entire life was an exposition of the power of faith in the Christ whom he loved and served.

Daily Chronicle, 25 July 1895 (reproduced from the *Wesleyan Methodist Monthly Greeting*, July 1895).

APPENDIX IV

A tribute to Revd H.V.P. Bronkhurst by Joseph Ruhomon, 18 July 1895

The Editor, *The Daily Chronicle*,

Sir, The death of the Rev. H.V.P. Bronkhurst must come as a shock to not a few of the people of British Guiana. Today, many like myself who have been accustomed to draw inspiration from him, and who have experienced his kindness and profited by his fatherly counsel which he was always so very ready and anxious to give, are inclined to cry out "a great man has fallen in Israel" and one whose place in society, made vacant by his vanished presence, it is so very difficult, nay, altogether impossible, to fill. I leave it to others to dwell on the public life and career of this good man who has left us, and made us poor indeed, by his departure from our midst. But as one who on several occasions has been privileged to sit by his side and to listen to his words of wisdom . . . words that have always inspired and nerved my heart, taking their rise, as they did, from a heart that throbbed with love and sympathy, I cannot refrain with [sic] the opportunity the sad occasion offers of publicly and gratefully acknowledging my greatest personal indebtedness to him. The late Mr. Bronkhurst has not only benefited me personally, but a large number of my East Indian friends in the Colony, who had come into direct contact with him. They have, in no mean measure, been influenced for good by the sweet, strong power exercised over them by the deceased gentleman, and it is chiefly owing to him that they today hold respectable positions in the Colony. A patriot he has always been and a great lover of his countrymen and their off-spring – the Hindo-Guianese, and the many and various attempts he had made to benefit them morally and socially, and the vast amount of real good he has been the means of achieving in endeavouring to better and ameliorate the conditions of East Indians in general in this Colony, will ever be a lasting and permanent memorial to his sterling character and solid worth as a man and a Christian worker . . .

Daily Chronicle, 21 July 1895.

APPENDIX V

"Coolie girl": "Aryan Kinswoman"?
An Englishman is enthralled by an Indo-Guyanese girl, Georgetown, ca. 1887

Strolling along the shady side of a wide and busy street, I overtook a young girl. I should have passed her, had I not slackened my gait when I came within a few steps of her; and, walking softly, measuring my paces by hers, followed behind the unknown wayfarer – respectfully and at a proper distance – to study and admire her costume, which was so neatly fitted to her slight and charming figure, so tastefully disposed, draped in such dainty folds and graceful gatherings, that the wearer of it made a most attractive picture.

Her little feet were bare; nevertheless she trod firmly, stepping lightly, with graceful poise, walking as only those women can walk who, all their lives innocent of high-heeled boots, learned to balance *bric-à-brac* on their heads when they were little, doll-cuddling girls. From time to time the maiden stopped to gaze into the shop-windows, viewing with eager, sparkling eyes the wonders, so attractive to her, displayed by drapers and dealers in fashionable stuffs. When she halted thus to feast her soul I passed ahead of her; then halting, waited till she, in turn, passed me again. In this way I was enabled to inspect, with approving criticism, the object of my admiration from tip to toe, and from every point of view. In time I made a mental catalogue of the bewildering items of her apparel and ornaments, taking memoranda that would enable an ingenious artist to paint from my description a full-length picture of her. Need I say I felt exceedingly diffident while following the young lady about the streets, and hesitated long before I ventured to open my note-book for the purpose of jotting down details of her word-picture I feared I might else forget. She caught me looking at her, and smiled quizzically, as if she found me grotesque or outlandish in appearance. Nevertheless she smiled, and I, taking heart of grace, whipped out my log and jotted down: "Teeth, regular, white" – and then, in admiration of her, I noted down as follows, as if I were filling the blank spaces of her passport: "Mouth, small and regular; lips, full and pouting; head, gracefully poised; face (mark this note, made in her gentle presence) – face, beautiful, oval, Grecian in type; nose, delicate, straight, finely chiselled (the last two words I must have cribbed from Ouida, one of whose intensest productions I had read on the voyage from Barbados); ears, small, well shaped, and *well put on;* hair, glossy, raven-black, straight and long, braided carefully with dexterous fingers, and tied at the ends with orange ribbons; hands, small, and covered with rings." *And now, alas! I must confess it – this Aryan kinswoman of mine was as brown as any Hindu cooly [sic] girl in Georgetown, and all of her East Indian sisters are as dusky as richest rosewood, as brown and dark as rarest mahogany.*

She was not a daughter of Ham nor child of Shem, but, like myself, a descendant of Father Japhet, a pure-blooded Hindu, albeit of low caste [emphasis added].

... A form
Of heavenly mould; a gait like Parvate's,
Eyes like a hind's in love-time, face so fair
Words cannot paint its spell.

Except for her sable colour she might have served for a study of a Caucasian beauty, for the model of a Grecian Psyche, an Italian contadina, a Gretchen, an English boarding-school miss, a freshwoman of Vassar. In her "finely chiselled nose" she wore a gold ring more than two inches in diameter. To keep this ornament from rudely meddling with her pouting lips, she fastened it back beside her cheek by means of a silver thread looped over her ear. She had four ear-rings in each ear – one, a large device of gold, hooked through the customary piercing in the lobe; the smaller three hanging in the outer rim. About her neck were coiled full half a score of necklaces of beaten silver, and pendant therefrom were numerous coins and charms of quaint devices. Upon her head there rested a silver coronet, from which small pieces of money, gold and silver, and some curious medallions, hung down upon her smooth brown brow. On every one of her eight taper fingers she wore two or more rings, and on each of her wee thumbs not less than half a dozen. There was such a mass of bracelets, bangles, and circlets around here wrists, I am within bounds when I say that three or four pounds in weight of sterling silver had been permanently withdrawn from circulation to be beaten and moulded for her ornamentation and adornment. Above her elbows, broad silver bands encircled her shapely arms, and tightly round her dark and silk-soft waist she had clasped a girdle, made by linking silver half-crowns and Spanish dollars together, all of which were fastened firmly to a broad belt of red leather.

My reader may now suppose that at last my catalogue of the metal-work with which this young Hindoo lady was weighted down, as if encased in armour, is completed. Not so, however; for on each and every unpinched toe of both her dusty, travel-stained, little feet there shone a gay, silver ring – wished on perhaps (romantic fancy!), by her own true love, who doubtless worshipped the very ground she trod upon. Nor will the list of this maiden's jewels be completed until I am permitted to mention that she wore massive golden, or gold-plated, anklets, so broad and heavy, so solid in appearance, that the astonished beholder might well wonder how she managed to walk and step so lightly. She wore a sleeveless jacket of red India silk, trimmed with narrow braids of gold lace. About her head was wrapped a veil of white, woven gauze, delicately embroidered with colored thread and fringed with knotted silk. The loose flowing continuations of this veil were wrapped and wreathed, festooned and garlanded, around her lissome form; but no man hath wit enough to tell, and no woman who has not practised the art from her cradle up can show, how gracefully and with what surprising dexterity this Hindoo girl managed the streamers of light cotton fabric. Deftly she controlled the flattering, misty length, now coiling it turban-shape upon her head, now binding it about her face to shield her from the sun, or, perhaps the too inquisitive gaze of passers-by. At times she hid her bare arms in its many folds, or, wreathing it about here neck, drew the ends around her waist; at times she looped it in front or knotted it behind her, and all this she did so easily, without apparent effort, and withal so unconsciously, it seemed as if she had but to wish the drifting cloud to wrap about and infold her, float behind or around her, and it obeyed, being governed by a breath, a sigh. The veil is to a Hindu girl what a fan is to a señorita of Castile. Deprive a Spanish beauty of her fan, the coolie belle of her veil, and both are ill at ease. They seem not to know what to do with their hands; they forget their airs and graces and coquettish ways; their toilet is incomplete and lacking in expression; the maids themselves are like birds with clipped wings.

I shall not attempt to describe how ethereal and sprite-like the coolie girl appeared to me; I was bewildered and bewitched as she tangled, entwined, interwove, and untwisted, yard upon yard of delicate film, all floating around her like a cloud of spray. Her skirts were of India muslin, soft and clinging, unflounced, and quite the reverse of trailing. All round about her lower borders were decorations of bright colors, embroidered with flowery brede of silken needle-work, and from beneath these scant phylacteries her little Hindu toes, all covered with rings, crept in and out like wee black mice in coats of silver mail. So soft were all her blended colorings, veiled in misty flutterings of cotton and fine silk, she lives in my memory, growing "in brightness, wearing her brilliant garment, the leader of the days, shining, gold-colored, lovely to behold – *Ushas*, Goddess of the Dawn." I lost sight at last of this Oriental vision; I do not choose to remember that she disappeared in mortal fashion, by prosaically turning a corner of the street – I prefer to indulge the fancy that she entered her private cloud, as Olympian goddesses of old were wont to do, and so was wafted away by the gentlest and floweriest of gales.

Later in the day, after I have recovered from the ecstasy and fever of regret of losing sight of the Hindu beauty, I was driven three miles from town to one of the most extensive sugar-estates in Demerara – in fact, in the world, where, in harvest time, there are nearly three thousand coolies employed.

William Agnew Paton, *Down the Islands: A Voyage to the Caribbee* (London: Kegan Paul, Trench and Co., 1888), 177–81.

APPENDIX VI

A retrospective by Joseph Ruhomon on the Indian condition in British Guiana, a quarter of a century after *India; The Progress of her People at Home and Abroad*

As far back as a quarter of a century ago . . . in a lecture in St. Leonard's schoolroom, Georgetown, I spoke in regretful terms of the backwardness of my race in this colony in the things that make for racial advancement and solidity, and threw out some practical suggestions which I thought might be helpful in this direction. A quarter of a century has gone by, and I do not see that the situation has improved to an extent reasonably proportionate to the length of time. The progress that should have been made has yet to be made . . .

I am glad to think, however, that in spite of the hindering elements at work, there is a good deal to the credit of the East Indian creoles. We find them in almost every sphere of life in the colony. The majority of them . . . find their means of subsistence in agricultural pursuits. Many of them are still attached to sugar plantations, and many of them find in rice planting a lucrative occupation, though adverse weather conditions often bring them serious reverses in fortune. Those who have gone in for stock-farming have done exceedingly well on the whole; and not a few can boast of vast possessions in flocks and herds, and in landed property. In trade and commerce they find a profitable field for their industry and their natural shrewdness; and in these pursuits their plodding, persevering habits never fail to bring them their reward. As book-keepers, panboilers, chemists and dispensers on sugar estates they are always in demand, and on no account for either of these offices where an East Indian creole is available will the service of any other nationality be engaged – so extremely careful and methodical are they and worthy of the confidence of their employers. As artisans and mechanics they can hold their own. They have proved their usefulness at works run by steam or electricity, and have shown a marked ability to master quickly the working of the most highly organised and intricate machinery. In the teaching profession they are thought well of by their managers and the Education authorities, and it is regrettable to think that in this important calling the pecuniary inducements are not such as to attract many more thereto.

In the Public Service the Government have seen the wisdom and expediency of employing East Indian creoles in various departments, thereby not only recognising, irrespective of nationality, but facilitating official business where illiterate Indians are concerned and eliminating the risk of possible misunderstanding and mistakes. The Judicial Establishment, the Treasury, the Medical Service, Postal Department, the Official Receiver's Office, have all gained more or less by such appointments.

In the professions, East Indian creoles are fairly well represented, and their number promises to be further augmented in the near future. Several of the youngsters have recently distinguished themselves in Queen's College and Berbice High School, one of them having actually carried off the Guiana Scholarship and is now at Oxford [Balgobin Persaud in 1916]. The Berbice High School [run by the Canadian Presbyterian Mission] – of which the Rev. J.A. Scrimgeour is principal – is proving more and more its immense usefulness and to an extent never anticipated when started as an ordinary primary school, and the exceptional advantages it offers are eagerly availed of by a large and increasing number of East Indians all over the county of Berbice. It is only to be hoped that the youngsters when out of training will think not so much of the two professions which in the eyes of East Indian parents constitute the *summum bonum* in earthly aspirations [law and medicine], but of the general wide field of human operations for which their minds are being trained and fitted under a system which aims at turning out good and useful citizens.

Believing that the future of the colony is largely in the hands of the East Indian creole, I should like to see him taking a greater and more active part in public affairs. His varied interests demand this. It should not all be shopkeeping and money making, while the higher interests of life are neglected. Efforts should be made on a well-organised and cooperative basis to work for all that will lift the race to a higher plane of thought and action [emphasis added]. It was for just such a purpose that the British Guiana East Indian Association was started [in New Amsterdam by Ruhomon in 1916], though selfish interests and party feeling have since been allowed to come in and it is today a house divided in itself. In a young community like ours and in such a narrow sphere of operations, I should not expect to see Gokhales and Gandhis and Tilaks in our midst; but I should expect to see at least some of the patriotic and self-sacrificing spirit of these men directed towards ends that shall compass every possible good demanding our attention and our efforts.

Joseph Ruhomon, 'The Creole East Indian", *Timehri*, 3rd ser., 7 (1921): 102, 104–6.

BIBLIOGRAPHY

PRIMARY SOURCES

Colonial Office Records
CO 111/606 Clementi to Bonar Law, no. 242, 15 July 1915.
CO 111/606 Clementi to Bonar Law, confidential, 15 July 1915.
CO 111/643 Collett to Churchill, no.161, 27 April 1922, enclosure. (Memorandum by J.A. Veerasawmy.)

Newspapers
Argosy (Georgetown, British Guiana), 1893–95; 1897; 1899–1900; 1904; 1906.
Berbice Gazette (New Amsterdam, British Guiana), 1894; 1900–1901.
Colonist (Georgetown, British Guiana), 1882.
Daily Argosy (Georgetown, British Guiana), 1920; 1922; 1942.
Daily Chronicle (Georgetown, British Guiana), 1894–96; 1930; 1939; 1942.

Reports
The Census Report of British Guiana, 1891; 1931.
Comins, D.W.D. *Note on Emigration from India to British Guiana*, (Diary). Calcutta: The Bengal Secretariat Press, 1893.
Report of the West India Royal Commission, 1897. H.W. Norman, chairman. London: HMSO, 1897.

SECONDARY SOURCES

Anon. *A Contribution to the History of Coolie Missions in British Guiana.* Georgetown: W.B. Jamieson, 1877.
Basham, A.L. *The Wonder that was India.* London: Sidgwick and Jackson, 1967 [1954].
Bronkhurst, H.V.P. *The Origin of the Guyanian Indians* . . . Georgetown, Demerara: The Colonist Press, 1881.
Bronkhurst, H.V.P. *The Colony of British Guyana [sic] and its Labouring Population.*

Bibliography

London: J. Woolmer, 1883.

Bronkhurst, H.V.P. *The Ancestry or Origin of our East Indian Immigrants; being an Ethnological and Philological Paper.* Georgetown: The Argosy Press, 1886.

Bronkhurst, H.V.P. *Among the Hindus and Creoles of British Guyana* [sic]. London: J. Woolmer, 1888.

Bronkhurst, H.V.P. *A Descriptive and Historical Geography of British Guiana and the West India Islands.* [Georgetown], Demerara: The Argosy Press, 1890.

Campbell, Jock. "Private Enterprise and Public Morality". *New Statesman*, 27 May 1966.

A Dictionary of Indian History. Calcutta: Calcutta University Press, 1967.

Fergusson, James. *History of Indian and Eastern Architecture.* London: John Murray, 1899 [1876].

Gist, Noel P. and Roy Dean Wright. *Marginality and Identity: Anglo-Indians as a Racially-Mixed Minority in India.* London: E.J. Brill, 1973.

Hanaford, Phebe A. *Daughters of America; or Women of the Century.* Boston: B.B. Russell, 1883.

Hargreaves, John D. *A Life of Sir Samuel Lewis.* London: Oxford University Press, 1958.

Hickerson, Harold. "Social and Economic Organisation in a Guiana Village". Ph.D. diss., University of Indiana, 1954.

Hooke, Fred W. *Life Story of a Negro Knight.* Freetown, Sierra Leone: The Author (?), 1915.

Hunter, W.W. *A Brief History of the Indian People.* London: Trubner and Co., 1882.

Laurence, K.O. *A Question of Labour: Indentured Immigration to Trinidad and British Guiana, 1875–1917.* Kingston, Jamaica: Ian Randle, 1994.

Look Lai, Walton. *Indentured Labour, Caribbean Sugar: Chinese and Indian Migrants to the British West Indies, 1838–1918.* Baltimore: Johns Hopkins University Press, 1993.

Mangru, Basdeo. *A History of East Indian Resistance on the Guyanese Sugar Plantations.* Lewiston, NY: The Edwin Mellen Press, 1996.

Masani, R.P. *Dadabhai Naoroji: The Grand Old Man of India.* London: George Allen and Unwin, 1939.

Mittelholzer, Edgar. *A Swarthy Boy.* London: Putnam, 1963.

Nath, Dwarka. *A History of Indians in Guyana.* London: The Author, 1970 [1950].

Nehru, Jawaharlal. *The Discovery of India.* London: Meridian Books, 1956 [1946].

O'Malley, L.S.S., ed. *Modern India and the West: A Study of the Interaction of Civilisations.* London: Oxford University Press, 1941.

Panikkar, K.M. *Essential Features of Indian Culture.* Bombay: Bharatiya Vidya Bhavan, 1964.

Parekh, Chunilal Lallabhai, ed. *Essays, Speeches, Addresses and Writings (on Indian Politics) of the Honourable Dadabhai Naoroji.* Bombay: Caxton Printing Works, 1887.

Paton, William Agnew. *Down the Islands: A Voyage to the Caribbees.* London: Paul, Trench and Co., 1888.

Ramabai Sarasvati, Pandita. *The High-Caste Hindu Woman.* Philadelphia: Press of the Jas. B. Rodgers Printing Co., 1887.

Bibliography

Ramcharitar-Lalla, C.E.J., ed. *Anthology of Local Indian Verse*. Georgetown: The Argosy Co., 1934.

Ramnarine, Tyran. "The Growth of the East Indian Community in British Guiana, 1880–1920". Ph.D. diss., University of Sussex, 1977.

Ramnarine, Tyran. "East Indian Political Representation in British Guiana during the Latter Part of Indenture", *Guyana Historical Journal* 2 (1990).

Raychaudhuri, Tapan. *Europe Reconsidered: Perceptions of the West in Nineteenth Century Bengal*. Delhi: Oxford University Press, 1988.

Rodney, Walter. *A History of the Guyanese Working People, 1881–1905*. Baltimore: Johns Hopkins University Press, 1981.

Ruhomon, Joseph. *India; The Progress of her People at Home and Abroad, and how Those in British Guiana may Improve Themselves*. Georgetown: C.K. Jardine, 1894.

Ruhomon, Joseph. "Reflections on the Season", *Berbice Gazette*, 25 December 1901.

Ruhomon, Joseph. "The Creole East Indian", *Timehri*, 3rd ser., 7 (1921).

Ruhomon, Joseph. *Signs and Portents: A Study of World Conditions and Prospects in the Light of Bible Prophecy*. New Amsterdam: Berbice Gazette Printing Press, [1921].

Ruhomon, Joseph. "Centenary Notes and Comments", *Indian Opinion* (Centenary Number) (1938).

Ruhomon, Peter. *Centenary History of the East Indians in British Guiana*. Georgetown: The East Indians 150th Anniversary Committee, 1988 [1947].

Samaroo, Brinsley. "The Indian Connection: The Influence of Indian Thought and Ideas on East Indians in the Caribbean". In *Indians in the Caribbean*, edited by I.J. Bahadur Singh. London: Oriental University Press, 1987.

Seecharan, Clem. *India and the Shaping of the Indo-Guyanese Imagination, 1890s-1920s*. Leeds: Peepal Tree Press, 1993.

Seecharan, Clem. *"Tiger in the Stars": The Anatomy of Indian Achievement in British Guiana, 1919–29*. London: Macmillan, 1997.

Seecharan, Clem. *Bechu: "Bound Coolie" Radical in British Guiana, 1894–1901*. Mona, Jamaica: The Press, University of the West Indies, 1999.

Temple, Richard. *India in 1880*. London: John Murray, 1880.

Temple, Richard. *Men and Events of my Time in India*. London: John Murray, 1882.

Who Is Who in British Guiana, 1935–37. Georgetown: Daily Chronicle Ltd, 1937.

Who Is Who in British Guiana, 1945–48. Georgetown: Daily Chronicle Ltd, 1948.

INDEX

Africa: legacy of ancient, 52–53; Ruhomon on the progress of, 50–53
African Association: founding of, x
Africans: progress of, in British Guiana, 5–66; Ruhomon on the progress of, 50–53; in the USA, 51–52
Afro-Guyanese: social mobility of, 5, 36 n.12
Ahmed, Sir Syed, 56, 57, 73 n.17
Aligarh Institute, 56, 57
Art: legacy of Indian, 74–75 n.24
Asiatic Cricket Club: formation of, 29, 42 n.81

Bechu, 7, 41 n.66; and culture of resistance, 25
Berbice Library: Revd H.J. Shirley and, 8
Blyden, Edward, x
British Guiana East Indian Association: purpose of, 92–93
British Guiana East Indian Cricket Club, 29
British Guiana East Indian Institute: founding of, 30
Bronkhurst, Revd H.V.P.: ambivalence towards India and Indians,13–17; arrival in British Guiana, 12; biographical note on,12–18; call for self-help society among Indians, 47; influence of, on Joseph Ruhomon, 11–12; introduction of, 47; on literary heritage of the Indians, 13; obituary of, 83–84; on Tamils, 40; tribute to, by Joseph Ruhomon, 85–86
Butcher, Basil, 29

Cameron, Norman: *Evolution of the Negro*, xi
Carpenter, Mary, 73 n.13
Centenary History, A.R.F. Webber, xi
Christian missionaries: and conversion of Indians, 13
Colonialism, British: denounced, x
Comins, D.W.D.: on situation of Indians, 26–27
"Coolie": use of the term, 2, 5, 18
Cricket: attachment of Indians to, 28–30; Prince Ranjitsinhji and, 30; symbolism of, in creole society, 29
Crowther, Bishop, 53
Crummell, Alexander, x
Culture of resistance: Bechu and, 25; among Indians, 24–26

Douglass, Frederick, 53, 72 n.8
Durham, F.A., x

"East Indian": explained, 71 n.2
East Indian Association, 56
East Indian Cricket Club, 30
East Indian Institute, 56, 69
Edun: achievements of, 27–28
Edun, Ayube: *London's Heart-Probe*, xi; and founding of trade union, 28

Index

Elvry, Ben: "To India", 63–64
Entrepreneurship: Indians and, 26
Evolution of the Negro, Norman Cameron, xi

Fazl, Abul, 74 n.22
Flood, Thomas, 30
Fredericks, Roy, 29
Froude, J.A., x

Guyana: intellectual resistance in, x–xi

Hawkins, Bishop Walter, 53
Headmaster: significance of position of, 36 n.12
Horton, James Africanus, x

India: the arts in, 59–60, 74–75 n.24; Ruhomon on independence for, 60; Ruhomon on reassertion of greatness of, 54–57; struggle for independence, ix
India; The Progress of Her People at Home and Abroad: challenge of, to stereotyping of Indians, 21; response of the Argosy to, 81–82; response of J.R. Wharton to, 79–80; retrospective by Ruhomon, 91–93; significance of, 2–3, 5
Indian indentureship: in the Caribbean, 2, 20
Indian National Congress: founding of, ix
Indians: as chemists and druggists, 35 n.7; condition of, in British Guiana, described, 64, 66–67; description of a woman, 87–90; entrepreneurship of, 26; founding of societies for self-interest, 30; images of, 20–21; intellectual achievements of, 31–32; literary heritage of, 13; as professionals in nineteenth century British Guiana, 2; in the professions, 61; qualities of, 62–63; Ruhomon on genius and industry of, 57–60; Ruhomon's retrospective on condition of, 91–93; Ruhomon on role for, in British Guiana, 92–93; sexual imbalance among indentured, 20; women as students, 61
Indians overseas: achievements of, 23

Jaundoo, F.E., 30
Jaundoo, Jacob, 41 n.75
Joshee, Anandibai, 75 n.30

Kallicharran, Alvin, 29
Kanhai, Rohan, 29
Karim, Hafiz Abdul, 23, 61
Keshab Chunder Sen, 73 n.13

Laurence, K.O.: on resistance on plantations, 40–41 n.64
Lewis, Sir Samuel, 53
London's Heart-Probe, Ayube Edun, xi
Love, Robert, x
Luckhoo, E.A., '31
Luckhoo, Joseph Alexander, 35 n.9
Luckhoo, Moses, 3; achievements of, 4; children of, 4; conversion to Christianity, 3
Lusitana Cricket Club, 29

Maceo, Antonio, x
Madray, Ivan, 29
Man Power Citizen's Association, xi
Mittelholzer, Edgar: and persona of the "coolie" in colonial society, 21
Moore, J.R., x
Morant Bay Rebellion, x

Naoroji, Dadabhai, 23, 61–62, 73 n.15, 76 n.32–34
National Indian Association: objectives of, 56, 73 n.13

Pahalad, 3; death of, 34 n.6; role of, in the family, 4
Pan-African Conference, x
Parents: responsibility of Indian, 68
Paton, William Agnew: description of an Indian woman, 87–90

Index

Permaul, J.W., 6
Persaud, Balgobin, 92
Press: Joseph Ruhomon on, 48
Professions: and social mobility, 5, 36 n.12
Progress: Joseph Ruhomon on, 49–53

Racism, 35–36 n.11; intellectual resistance to European, ix–x
Roy, Ram Mohan, 12, 73 n.13
Ramaswami, Mr.: poem of, 60
Ramnarine, Tyran, 15
Ranjitsinhji, Prince: rise of, in cricket, 30, 42 n.84, 85
Resistance. *See* Culture of resistance
Rice cultivation: among Indians, 26
Ruhomon, John, 3–4; conversion to Christianity, 3; missionaries' influence on, 3; proficiency in Indian languages, 3–4
Ruhomon, Joseph, ix; on Africans in the USA, 51–52; biographical note, 3–10; Christian principles of, 9; on the development of the intellect, 23–24; early influences on, 7–9; on eminence of ancient Africa and India, 22; exhortation to Indians in British Guiana, 70; on independence for India, 60; *India; The Progress of Her People at Home and Abroad*, 2, 3, 5, 6, 48–70, 71 n.1; Indianness of, 17; on Indians in British Guyana, 6; on Indo-Guyanese in the 1890s, 22–23; influence of H.V.P. Bronkhurst on, 11–12; as intellectual, 2; on intellectual progress of Indo-Guyanese, 31; on intellectual stature of Afro-Guyanese, 22; journalistic work of, 9; on knowledge, 50; lack of prejudice of, 24; pamphlets published, 8; on progress, 49–53; on progress of Africa and Africans, 50–53; on reassertion of India, 54–57; retrospective by, on condition of Indians, 91–93; on role for Indians in British Guiana, 92–93; tribute of, to Revd H.V.P. Bronkhurst, 85–86; tribute to, 32–33; and use of term "coolie", 18
Ruhomon, Peter, 5; and tribute to Joseph Ruhomon, 32–33

Sarasvati, Pandita Ramabai, 75 n.29
Scholes, T.E.S., x
Sharples, Loris Rohan: racial prejudice against, 35–36 n.11
Shirley, Revd H.J.: and the Berbice Library, 8
Social mobility: the professions and, 5, 36 n.12
Societies: benefits of, 69–70; lack of, for Indians in British Guiana, 68–70
Society for the Encouragement and Preservation of Indian Art, 57
Solomon, Joe, 29

Tamils: H.V.P. Bronkhurst on, 40
Temple, Sir Richard, 56, 73 n.16
Thomas, J.J., x
"To India", Ben Elvry, 63–64
Trim, John, 29

United States of America (USA): Ruhomon on Africans in, 51–52

Veerasawmy, J.A., 29
Veerasawmy, Mudaliar, 30
Vivekananda, Swami, 23, 77

Webber, A.R.F.: *Centenary History*, xi
Whites: racial arrogance of, in British Guiana, 24
Williams, Henry Sylvester: and founding of the African Association, x
Williams, Revd J.E.S., 12
Wharton, James, 30
Wharton, J.R.: on *India; The Progress of Her People at Home and Abroad*, 79–80
Wharton, William Hewley: achievements of, 30–31

www.ingramcontent.com/pod-product-compliance
Lightning Source LLC
Chambersburg PA
CBHW020831190426
43197CB00037B/1477